CW00545905

With Recce at Arnhem

With Recce at Arnhem

The Recollections of Trooper Des Evans – A 1st Airborne Division Veteran

Mike Gallagher

Pen & Sword
MILITARY

First published in Great Britain in 2015 by
Pen & Sword Military
an imprint of
Pen & Sword Books Ltd
47 Church Street
Barnsley
South Yorkshire
S70 2AS

Copyright © Mike Gallagher 2015

ISBN 978 1 47384 363 9

The right of Mike Gallagher to be identified as the Author of this
Work has been asserted by him in accordance with the Copyright,
Designs and Patents Act 1988.

A CIP catalogue record for this book is available from the British
Library

All rights reserved. No part of this book may be reproduced or
transmitted in any form or by any means, electronic or mechanical
including photocopying, recording or by any information storage
and retrieval system, without permission from the Publisher in
writing.

Typeset in Ehrhardt by
Mac Style Ltd, Bridlington, East Yorkshire
Printed and bound in the UK by CPI Group (UK) Ltd,
Croydon, CRO 4YY

Pen & Sword Books Ltd incorporates the imprints of Pen &
Sword Archaeology, Atlas, Aviation, Battleground, Discovery,
Family History, History, Maritime, Military, Naval, Politics,
Railways, Select, Transport, True Crime, and Fiction, Frontline
Books, Leo Cooper, Praetorian Press, Seaforth Publishing and
Wharncliffe.

For a complete list of Pen & Sword titles please contact
PEN & SWORD BOOKS LIMITED
47 Church Street, Barnsley, South Yorkshire, S70 2AS, England
E-mail: enquiries@pen-and-sword.co.uk
Website: www.pen-and-sword.co.uk

Contents

List of Plates   vi
Introduction to With Recce at Arnhem   viii
Prologue: Strange Meeting   xiii

Chapter 1   Return to Arnhem 1984   17

Chapter 2   Joining the Airborne Brotherhood   14

Chapter 3   Ruskington   18

Chapter 4   Wings   26

Chapter 5   Lead Up to Operation Market Garden   33

Chapter 6   Departure for Arnhem: Sunday, 17 September 1944   39

Chapter 7   Monday, 18 September 1944   45

Chapter 8   Tuesday, 19 September 1944   49

Chapter 9   Arnhem Aftermath   56

Chapter 10   Apeldoorn and Amersfoort   60

Chapter 11   Destination Germany   64

Chapter 12   Journey's End; Frankfurt-Am-Main   70

Chapter 13   Stalag XIIA Limburg   77

Chapter 14   Stalag IVB Mühlberg   84

Chapter 15   Borna   95

Chapter 16   March to Freedom   112

Chapter 17   Escape and Freedom   116

Epilogue   133

List of Plates

'R' Reserve Troop 1st Airlanding Reconnaissance Squadron, Ruskington, Lincolnshire, taken in July 1944 before the Evrecy (Caen) briefing – one of the many planned, then cancelled, operations involving 1st Airborne Division prior to Arnhem.

The famous photograph taken by Sergeant Mike Lewis AFPU, on the Deutskampfsweg, Wolfheze, 18 September 1944.

The Grave of Trooper Bill Edmond of the 1st Airborne Reconnaissance Squadron, KIA 17 September 1944.

Studio portrait of Des Evans, taken in Liverpool in 1945 while he was on PoW leave.

Des Evans in an informal pose at Aberystwyth in 1952, whilst serving with a TA anti-aircraft regiment.

Des Evans on the historic DZ at Ginkel Heath in September 1984, wearing the original beret that he wore at Arnhem in 1944.

Des Evans and friends in 1986 at the scene where the now famous photograph was taken.

Des Evans in conversation with General Sir John Hackett, following the 'silent march to the Arnhem Bridge', September 1986.

Des Evans taking part in the Remembrance Sunday parade, Sherringham 1992.

The grave of Trooper Jimmy Salmon of the 1st Airborne Reconnaissance Squadron, KIA 19 September 1944.

The grave of Trooper Fred Brawn of the 1st Airborne Reconnaissance Squadron, KIA 19 September 1944.

The grave of Corporal Alan Baker of the 1st Airborne Reconnaissance Squadron, KIA 19 September 1944.

The last resting place of Trooper Bill Edmond of the 1st Airborne Reconnaissance Squadron, KIA 17 September 1944.

Des at the Hartenstein Hotel on his first return visit to Arnhem in 1984.

Des Evans wearing the beret he wore at Arnhem and in captivity, Remembrance Sunday parade, Sherringham 1992.

Vehicles of the Reconnaissance Squadron Living History Group parked at the actual site of the Amsterdamsweg ambush, during the sixtieth anniversary commemorations, 2004.

Members of the Norfolk Branch of the Parachute Regiment Association assemble to pay a last farewell to Des at his funeral in July 2010.

Mr Nick Clark, Standard Bearer for the Reconnaissance Squadron Old Comrades Association, standing in front of the wreath sent by the association.

Introduction to *With Recce at Arnhem*

With 2014 marking the 70th anniversary of the Battle of Arnhem/Oosterbeek – that magnificent yet tragic enterprise to capture the road bridge over the Rhine in September 1944, it seems opportune to offer those interested in studying the battle a personal account of that battle which has never before been read in its entirety. Much has already been written on the subject, from individual participant accounts of the battle, to grand overviews of both the strategic and operational consequences of the engagement and its wider impact on the Allied offensive in the west. It is not my intention to provide yet another overview of the Battle of Arnhem/Oosterbeek, for the reader unfamiliar with it – and who seeks to discover more – I would direct their reading to Martin Middlebrook's seminal work *Arnhem – The Airborne Battle*, Robert Jackson's *Arnhem – The Battle Remembered*, and John Fairley's *Remember Arnhem*, all of which provide a good background to the activities at Arnhem/Oosterbeek around which this account is based. Should the reader wish to visit the battlefield, I would further recommend Frank Steer's *Arnhem – The Landing Grounds*, published by Pen and Sword.

This is the account of an ordinary man – if a participant and survivor of that epic battle can be deemed ordinary – a Trooper in the 1st Airlanding Reconnaissance Squadron. He wrote his account – like many veterans of the battle – long after the war whilst in retirement. In fact he did not begin to commit his account to paper until after his first visit to Arnhem since the battle, in 1984, forty years later. The very act of writing it down was a painful yet cathartic experience as he had spoken little of his experiences to anyone before 1984. Despite the intervening years, his incredible powers of recollection and detail are evident throughout. This account or odyssey begins with his return to Arnhem in 1984 and then takes us on his journey of joining 'Recce', parachute training, Arnhem and finally his captivity and eventual escape from captivity.

Like many young men in 1944 Desmond Fredrick Charles Evans came from humble origins. He was brought up in pre-war Walton, Liverpool by a hard-working family. His mother 'Emma' sewed for a living whilst his father 'Fredrick' (ex Royal Navy and the winner of a Mention in Despatches at Jutland – having dragged a wounded comrade from a burning deck) worked initially selling insurance 'door to door' and latterly for Vernons Pools. He was the middle of three children – he had an elder sister Beryl and a younger brother Walter or Wally. As a high-spirited and somewhat rebellious youngster, Desmond had brushed up against authority which had lead to 'a summons before the Magistrate' and a fine at 11 years old and later a spell in Borstal (an experience he was never to forget). He'd left school at 14 years without qualifications to work in one of the many pre-war labour schemes designed to ensure the youth of the day were properly employed. That work was labouring on a farm near Ormskirk in Lancashire. Although Des had no formal qualifications or ever undertook any further education post war, he wrote his account with a fluent and engaging hand; he was self-taught and could turn his hand to most things. He had a wealth of life experiences and that ultimate gift… common sense. He was able to hold conversations and correspond with former generals, private soldiers, renowned authors and military historians with equal ease and finesse; either party would be captivated by his word craft and ability to communicate.

When war came Des was considered to be in a Reserved Occupation; he was thus prevented from initially enlisting. However, eager to do his bit he joined the fledgling Home Guard. Repeated efforts to enlist came to naught, so eventually – being an enterprising chap and realizing the problem was the reserved occupation – he absconded from his new employer (a farm in Derbyshire) made his way to the recruiting centre in Derby, told the Recruiting Staff he was unemployed… and he was in! He was sent to Richmond and the Depot of the Green Howards. He was a natural soldier, who enjoyed soldiering; as a consequence he was retained at the Depot as part of a 'Demonstration Squad' for new recruits. Keen to be *in* the war and not sitting it out, he volunteered for the newly created Reconnaissance Corps.

Des completed his Corps training, and having learned to ride a motorcycle he was posted to North Africa as a Despatch Rider. After the Afrika Corps defeat in North Africa in 1943 – and his many adventures in the desert – his unit took part in the operations in Sicily and Italy, following the landings there. It was during that bitterly cold winter of 1943/44 amongst the hills of southern Italy, that he contracted pneumonia. Des was evacuated sick back to England and after recovering was sent to convalesce at Middleton Towers Camp near Morecambe in Lancashire. When he had recovered fully he found himself without a parent unit (his was still overseas), and on discovering that the 1st Airlanding Reconnaissance Squadron needed reinforcements having returned from the Mediterranean theatre, he volunteered for Airborne Forces, was accepted, attended selection and training at Hardwick Hall, Parachute Training at Ringway and was posted to Reserve Troop at Ruskington in Lincolnshire. It was by a mere twist of fate that Des was even at the legendary battle of Arnhem/Oosterbeek: a comrade injured in an impromptu football kick about, meant he was selected (or rather detailed) to take the man's place. As such he was allocated as a replacement to 'C' Troop 1st Airlanding Reconnaissance Squadron.

After his repatriation from PoW Camp in April 1945, he returned to his home town of Liverpool on leave. He met his first wife; however it wasn't to be a happy match and perhaps realizing there was no future in the marriage, he opted to continue soldiering.

He served in Trieste, Palestine, Germany, the UK and latterly Egypt on the Suez Canal when he was re-mobilized on the 'Z' Reserve for Korea. He finally left the Regular Army in 1954 with the rank of sergeant.

He submitted his account to Martin Middlebrook on request (veterans accounts were being sought), prior to his book's release in 1994. Although acknowledged in the book, none of Des's account was used in *Arnhem – The Airborne Battle*. Robert Jackson did however use some excerpts of Des's story in his book *Arnhem – The Battle Remembered*, which was also released in 1994 in time for the 50th anniversary of the battle. However, apart from a few of these previously published excerpts, the remainder of the material in this book in connection with the battle and Des's subsequent incarceration is fresh to the market having never been published before.

Sadly Des died in 2010 aged 86 years (3 months after his beloved wife and companion Betty to whom he was devoted). That most cruel of diseases 'Dementia' had destroyed what had been Des and he finished his days alone in a Home for those suffering from Enduring Mental Illness. Because of his advanced dementia it was not possible for him to spend the remainder of his days with Betty, so they died apart. In 2013 I attended the interment of Betty and Des's Ashes. After the service, all of his extensive archive and memorabilia was given into my care. This is my tribute to a much loved and admired friend and mentor.

This is *his story,* in *his words* of three days of absolute hell in the cauldron of Oosterbeek – he never got to the Bridge at Arnhem. Those three days were followed by eight months of enduring hell as an enforced guest in Hitler's Third Reich.

Prologue: Strange Meeting

Since I was a small boy I have had a fascination for history and in particular military history. My bedroom walls were covered with prints of Waterloo, Balaklava, Rorke's Drift and Arnhem. What wall space remained was equally adorned with swords, medals, badges and helmets. One battle that particularly fascinated me was the battle of Arnhem. My father had lost a friend there serving with the 3rd Battalion Parachute Regiment. In the 1970s I eagerly consumed any and every account of the battle I could obtain, which culminated in my being taken by my father to watch that classic war film *A Bridge Too Far*, a truly memorable experience for me.

I joined the Territorial Army at 17 and began to get a better understanding of soldiering albeit part-time and in peace time; the camaraderie, hardships and 'fun' of soldiering. I would get a much deeper understanding of the raw horror of war twenty-seven years later whilst serving in a Field Hospital in Afghanistan on Operation Herrick 14. At 19, together with two good friends (equally interested in military history), we made the journey to Holland in September 1984 for the 40th anniversary of the battle of Arnhem.

As was usual in those days, we caught the train to Harwich. This was budget travel and our overnight *luxury* accommodation was the reclining chair. Unfortunately, having spent too long at the bar, we found ourselves locked out of the reclining chair lounge. We therefore resigned ourselves to an uncomfortable night sleeping on the floor near one of the inner stair-wells – but we were young.

As we settled down I noticed an elderly chap with untidy white hair and a check jacket, asleep on a convenient couch. This wasn't particularly remarkable; what was remarkable was the very attractive young lady who was sharing the couch with him, top to tail. I nudged my friends and recall making the comment 'lucky old sod'. We speculated that he was some sort of sugar daddy or Svengali.

We docked the following morning at the Hook of Holland and caught the train to Arnhem. Once there we proceeded to hire bicycles, book into a cheap hotel (remarkably easy given the fact that there were over 1,500 veterans attending the pilgrimage). We cycled up to Oosterbeek, paid our respects at the Arnhem/Oosterbeek War Cemetery, including laying a tribute on the grave of my father's friend. We visited the Hartenstein Hotel which had been 1st Airborne Divisional Headquarters during the battle, and my friend even found an unfired 1944-dated British 9mm round in the woods at the back of the hotel!

We were in the entrance of the Hartenstein Hotel. My friend Pete had bought a new 'print' of the battle and had decided to get it signed by as many Arnhem veterans as he could ask. We saw a small figure wearing a red beret in conversation with a Dutchman. We approached and apologized for eavesdropping and asked the obvious question, 'excuse me, but did you fight at Arnhem?' I suppose the chap must have thought we were Dutch, however once he heard our accents (we are all from the North of England) he at once engaged us in conversation in an accent which had the detectable lilt of a Liverpudlian:

'Yes, I was with Recce at Arnhem!'

Whilst this gentleman was chatting to us, it suddenly dawned on me that this was the old boy asleep on the couch with the attractive young lady, so I asked him if it was him and where she was.

He grinned and admitted that it was him and that he had simply asked to share the couch with her as he too had no chair to sleep on. She saw no objection, so they had cuddled up together for a comfortable night's sleep (certainly more conducive and comfortable than ours had been).

We introduced ourselves and of course Des Evans introduced himself. He explained that he had recently been made redundant (he was 61 years old at the time) and that he and his wife had used his redundancy money to renovate their medieval thatched cottage in Gloucestershire. They had then sold it to move to a smaller property at West Runton, Norfolk in order to liberate some money which they invested in an Income Bond. Des had mentioned to Betty that it was the 40th anniversary and she had insisted he make the effort for his first pilgrimage since the battle. Being cognisant of the need to save money, Des at 61 had donned his airborne red beret and had literally hitchhiked from West Runton to Harwich and from the Hook of Holland to Oosterbeek. He had spent his first night at a youth hostel. However, he had been approached by a gentleman called Tanno Peterson who was responsible for providing 'Host' accommodation for veterans as part of the 'Lest We Forget Foundation'. Because Des had never been back to Arnhem and because of the real possibility that he might be someone hoping to 'bask in the glory', his bonifides were therefore carefully checked and confirmed, and a suitable 'Host' was found for Des for the duration of his stay. We insisted on taking Des for a drink and a meal and slowly he began to tell us the story of his part in the battle of Arnhem/Oosterbeek. One element that stands out is the battered press cutting he kept in his wallet. It was of a well-known photograph taken at Wolfheze around 18 September 1944.

In the photograph there is a PIAT gunner lying prone and a Rifleman with No 4 Rifle and Bayonet in the kneeling alert position. In the background you see another individual with a Bren gun. Des said, 'that's me with the rifle and bayonet, the PIAT gunner is Jimmy Cooke and the Bren Gunner is Fred Brawn who was killed.' I'd seen the photograph dozens of times; I couldn't believe I was meeting someone actually in that photograph and I never once doubted his sincerity.

Des made a lasting impression on me and I suppose I must have equally made an impression on him. We exchanged addresses and phone numbers and I promised to make contact as soon as we returned. We parted, and I know that all of us were extremely moved by his story – myself in particular.

We returned home to the UK, and I wrote to Des. Very promptly I received a reply with an invitation to visit him and his wife at their cottage in West Runton. We agreed a weekend and I went. I had a wonderful weekend and Betty and Des were the perfect hosts. We talked well into the wee small hours and by the end of my visit I was genuinely sorry to be leaving and a bond that would endure had been forged. Not only had I befriended a genuine Arnhem Veteran, he even signed my battered copy of *Remember Arnhem* which I left with him to read and critique. I had made a friend who would be a mentor, whose regard for me was unconditional, and who in many respects was the perfect father figure.

My own father (only three years junior to Des), had himself seen service towards the end of the war, yet whereas he would be critical towards my supposed many failings, Des would be considerate and caring. Where my father would be decidedly unenthusiastic about my plans and achievements, Des would encourage and offer wise council. No more was this true than when in the late 1980s I volunteered for a Basic Parachute course at JSPC Netheravon, I told my own father – who had been with the 6th Airborne Division himself – who gave the following negative response: 'you'll get yourself bloody killed.'

However, that of Des was the opposite, providing encouragement, advice and when I visited him before the course, he leant me his battered old red beret (the one in fact that he had worn at Arnhem and through captivity) as a talisman to put into my smock. I recall his words now: 'I can't be with you – I wish I could – so take a little part of me to be with you.' I did, and successfully – and safely – completed the course.

Over the years, Des painstakingly began to open up and tell his story. With some encouragement from me I suggested he should write it down. He not only wrote down his story of the battle at Oosterbeek, but also of his early military service, of his captivity after the battle, and much later his entire life story which was full of triumph and disaster. One thing is for certain: whatever might have happened in his life, I recognized him as an intrinsically good man; it was not for me to judge, and his honesty made me respect him all the more.

Here then is Des Evans's own story, from joining airborne forces, his part in the action at Oosterbeek in 1944, and his subsequent captivity. Where necessary, and to clarify any point of historical accuracy, I have (where possible) included accompanying notes. This is my tribute to you old friend, may you rest in peace!

Chapter One

Return to Arnhem 1984

My name is Desmond Evans, but known to everyone simply as Des. I thought that having reached the age of sixty-one my adventures were well and truly over; however, the fourteenth of September 1984 was the date when I began what was, for me, a most incredible experience. As Betty (my wife) was still recovering from her recent operation we both felt that I alone should still make a special effort to go to Arnhem. It was an unusual occasion because it was the fortieth anniversary of the battle, and I had never been back there since it took place.

The cost of taking my motor caravan over there just for me was rather too much, so I decided to hitch-hike. Yes, at sixty-one I felt that getting on the road was the only way I was going to get to Arnhem. I must admit that I did start my journey by getting the local train from West Runton to Norwich, but after that it was hitch-hike all the way (except for the sea crossing of course). I had the most extraordinary luck with my lifts because each time I was picked up, within minutes it started to rain heavily. Three vehicles picked me up this side, a car, a lorry and a van. The van driver was going over as a foot passenger on the boat, so he took me right into the ferry terminal. The boat journey was uneventful – I'd made a point of catching the night boat so that I would arrive there in daylight. I had hoped to get off the boat at the Hook of Holland quickly so that, using my card with the word 'ARNHEM' in large letters I would be in the right place when all the cars came off. It didn't work out like that though. There was such a long delay getting through passport control, that by the time I got away from there all the cars had gone. However, I started walking with my pack on my back and my sleeping bag in a zipped holdall and within minutes a Dutch lorry driver picked me up and took me within fifteen miles of Arnhem via Rotterdam.

Again I started hiking and must say that I walked further than I'd bargained for, about five miles in fact. By this time the rain was coming down gently and I thought that as I had my old red beret in my pocket I might as well put it on, first of all to keep off the rain and secondly in the hope that it might get me a lift. It worked on both counts! A car pulled up, an English car driven by an ex-paratrooper who was on his way to Arnhem too. He greeted me with the words, 'you must be going to the same place as me'. In short, he drove me into the town and, having plenty of time before booking into his hotel, he asked me where I would like to go. The cemetery seemed to be a good place to begin, so that's where we went. I stood over the grave of one of my dead comrades and thanked him for forty years' bonus of life, because just a few minutes before my Jeep was ambushed forty years earlier I'd asked him to change places with me on the Jeep; he agreed, and now it's he who is lying in the cemetery and not me. Fate indeed plays strange tricks does it not?

Reg Isherwood, the chap who picked me up, was talking to a couple of young Dutch chaps when I rejoined him and it seemed that they were interested in getting personal stories of the battle. They planned to write a book of anecdotes gathered in this way. I produced the picture of myself that was taken during the battle and they were immediately fascinated by it. Opening the book they were carrying, they showed me a copy of the same picture and got me to autograph the page under the photo. The Dutch chaps then asked where we would like to go as they were prepared to take us anywhere.

We both said we'd like to go to Wolfheze, close to the LZ (Landing Zone for Gliders), to the DZ (Dropping Zone for paratroops), and also to where the news correspondent had taken the photo. This they did and although it all looked familiar to me, I couldn't orientate myself to the point of recognizing points of interest.

We drove back into Oosterbeek just outside Arnhem, where most of the fighting took place and I said, 'I'd like to go to the museum there.' It's housed in the building that was used as the Divisional HQ in 1944. The Dutch chaps left us there saying that they would be back in an hour. I walked in wearing my old red beret and almost immediately a chap threw his arms around me, 'Des Evans', he said, 'Don't you know me?' It was one of my old friends I hadn't seen for forty years, but he recognized me. It was George Bell, but he had changed so much I must confess that I didn't recognize him. We had quite a chat as you can imagine. It was while we were talking that I realized that the chaps who had said they would come back in an hour had driven away with my kit. Anyway, not to worry, they did come back with the good news that they had found me an address to take me to. This they proceeded to do. On the way out I had a word with the curator. 'The' photograph was, as I'd anticipated, in the museum, a larger copy on the wall, and of the three men shown only one was named…Jimmy Cooke. I gave them my name, but couldn't remember the name of the third man in the photograph at that time. For forty years all I could remember was that his name began with the letter 'B'. He too had been killed on my Jeep.

The Dutch lads took me to the house of a member of the 'Lest We Forget' Committee, and she fixed me up with a bed at the youth hostel just outside the town.

So that's where I spent my first night and, tired though I was, I took the bus into Arnhem proper to have a good look at the bridge that the fuss was all about in 1944. The following morning, Sunday, I visited the cemetery again and, as I'd anticipated, Reg Isherwood was there, talking to a large Dutchman. I was looking round the graves again when suddenly I saw a name that I instantly recognized – 'F BRAWN' – and I knew that this was the name of the other chap in the picture, at last after forty years. You will appreciate that all of this was extremely emotional for me.

I went across to join Reg and the chap he was talking to. He was a very big man over six feet tall and I saw that he was wearing the tie of my old unit the 1st Airborne Reconnaissance Squadron. I showed him the badge in my beret which I was carrying. It turned out that he was one of the Dutch commandos attached to my unit for the operation in Holland. I asked him if he knew what happened to the other commando who was attached directly to my Troop (C Troop) and was told that he was dead, having died from natural causes two or three years ago. He insisted on taking us home for a drink. We got into his car and he drove us to a pleasant suburb of Oosterbeek. As we approached his house he pointed out a piece of ground that was being cleared for the building of another house. 'They started levelling that space two weeks ago', he said, 'and found two bodies, or what remained of them.' They were the bodies of two paratroopers who had died in the battle and after forty years were found. The authorities go to extraordinary lengths to identify them. Their dog-tags were missing, but the Dutch hoped to identify them by their teeth amongst other things.

We had a very pleasant time with the Dutchman and his family and whilst we were there I was shown a copy of a book, *Remember Arnhem* by John Fairley, and it's entirely about the role my unit played during the battle. Once again 'my picture' showed up; it was on the cover. I had no idea such a book existed and must try to get a copy.

'Pim', the Dutchman, ran us back into the centre of Oosterbeek and I said 'cheerio' to Reg as he was going home the following day. I then went into the museum again and this time told the curator the name of the third man in the photograph. He thanked me very warmly and said he could now bring the caption up to date. While I was telling him this, three English lads came up to me and were listening to what I had to say. When I'd finished talking to the curator, they apologized for eavesdropping and then asked me if I would sign a picture print of the battle they had just bought.

They were young chaps who, being fascinated by all they'd heard and read about Arnhem, had decided to come over and look around. They had hired bikes for the day but then opted to walk around with me asking questions about what had happened forty years ago. I spent a very pleasant afternoon with them and before leaving them I gave them my address. Imagine my surprise when, on arriving home, I found that they had sent Betty a postcard saying that they had met me and that I was safe. There was also a letter from one of them asking if he could come here to visit me, this was Mike. I was flattered; I must have made a good impression, one supposes. When I parted from them I assumed it was 5 o'clock and therefore had plenty of time to get back to the hostel for my evening (main) meal. However, I soon realized that it was in fact 6 o'clock as I hadn't put my watch on continental time. There was no way I could get back to the hostel for 6.30pm; this was when they stopped serving, so I just went into a nearby café and ordered a meal and a drink. There I met another old friend from the unit, Bill Bateman with his wife and sister and brother-in-law.

Again we nattered about many things; this was emotional too, and I ended up literally crying on his wife's shoulder. I had kept it all pent up until then. I suppose it just had to come out sooner or later.

Monday, 17 September 1984, I attended the wreath-laying ceremony at the huge monument at Oosterbeek opposite the Hartenstein Hotel having walked from the youth hostel. I was talking before the service to a chap in a wheelchair; he asked me how I had got to Arnhem and where I was staying. Assuming that he was just making polite conversation I told him. After the ceremony, which was short and simple, with the 'Last Post' being played at the end of it, I was approached by an English speaking Dutchman who introduced himself as Tanno Peterson and asked if I'd like to spend the rest of the day with him. Of course I readily agreed. I had nothing planned for the remainder of the day, so off I went with him, accompanied by his attractive second wife.

We went to many places that day because Tanno is totally committed to the 'Lest We Forget' Committee. One place he insisted on taking me to was Wolfheze and this time we found the exact spot where the famous picture had been taken. We also went over the route of the patrol on which my Jeep was ambushed; everything came back to me with tremendous impact. I had to ask Tanno to stop the car for a little while to get myself together; I had to tell myself it all happened forty years ago.

We went to his home where his wife cooked us a meal. Tanno dialled my home number and I was able to talk to Betty and tell her what had happened thus far.

He also told me how thrilled he was to have me in his house and that later we would collect my kit from the hostel, as he had found a 'Host Home' for me. These quarters are provided solely by Dutch people offering their homes to veterans like myself. I was extremely lucky with mine, a young couple, Josie and Peter Van Nordern. They put me up, fed me, even gave me a key to the door, showed me where everything was kept so that I could feed myself if I came in when they were at work, and generally made me feel very welcome. We got on very well together and made each other laugh a lot.

When I had been in the cemetery on Sunday 16 September I had a brief conversation with an English couple, who came into the cemetery behind me. The wife asked me how I had got to Arnhem, so I smiled and gave the 'thumbing motion' of the hitch-hiker. 'What'? she said, 'Do you mean you hitched?' 'Yes', I said. Her husband said – rather vehemently – 'You're not bloody going back like that, you're coming back with us!' There and then we made arrangements for the meeting a week on Tuesday so that I could travel back with them. So, all the kindness didn't come from the Dutch.

Whilst meeting the Polish contingent with Tanno I got into conversation with a young Dutch Airforce Officer. 'Why don't you come on the trip to the Hague tomorrow?' he said to me. So Tuesday, 18 September found me at 9 o'clock in the morning boarding one of two coaches bound for the capital for the State Opening of Parliament by their Queen. They treated us like royalty. It was absolutely marvellous. We were given coffee and cake on our arrival, and then taken outside to a specially allocated space from where we saw the procession and the bands and finally their Queen in her golden couch. She turned and waved to us because she had been told we were there.

A really smashing occasion, the weather too was kind; from rain early in the morning it turned into a beautiful day. We all then went inside again where speeches were made and when the Polish spokesman stood up to make his speech of thanks in English, I was thinking that I was the new boy there and felt that someone else would surely speak up for the British contingent. No one did, however, so guess who volunteered? Yes, Des Evans made a short speech of thanks to the Dutch Parliament. How about that? The visit was concluded by our being given lunch and I had my photo taken with an American General by a Polish chap who wanted a picture of an English paratrooper with an American paratrooper and two Polish paras. We were all presented with a special medal and a tie made for the occasion too.

There was a coach trip of the battlefield planned for Wednesday, 19 September and I had been introduced, by Tanno, to another Dutch chap who spoke excellent English and who was going on this tour with me because he wanted to see exactly where my photo had been taken at Wolfheze in 1944. I was standing waiting for the coach when I saw another of my old mates. We got to talking; I produced the picture yet again saying: 'That's me, that's Jimmy Cooke and that's Fred Brawn'. Right away he said, 'Fred's brother is over there, I'll go and get him'.

Within seconds, it seemed, I was shaking hands with Arthur Brawn, tears streaming down our faces and me saying, 'I don't know what to say to you Arthur'. However, we recovered and there I was talking to Fred's brother who had been looking for forty years for someone to tell him how his brother had died at Arnhem.

I was able to tell him and assure him that Fred had not suffered, that he had in fact died very quickly and was not in any way disfigured either. We got onto the coaches and started our tour and when we reached the spot in Wolfheze where the picture was taken everyone got off the six coaches. I was surrounded by dozens of people and was showing the picture round, as I had been asked to do. Then instead of the question and answer session I had anticipated, this Dutch fellow thrust a loud hailer into my hand and asked me to tell them all about the story behind the photograph. It threw me off balance for a moment, but I got myself together and managed to tell the crowd all that had taken place. There were gasps when I told them how close I had come to being killed and had only avoided it by changing places with a friend on the Jeep. There were further gasps when I introduced Arthur as the brother of another man killed on my Jeep. After the tour I spent the rest of the day with Arthur and his wife Rene. I could see that my story cheered them to some extent and the day ended far more happily than it had begun.

The big event planned for Thursday, 20 September 1984 was the inauguration of the Eusebius Church in Arnhem; destroyed in the battle it had been beautifully rebuilt. It was not a service as such, but a well-balanced programme which included music from the Dutch Airforce band, and songs, including 'Land of Hope and Glory' sung by an English woman who was married to a Dutchman. She had a lovely voice, her name was Caroline Kaart. There was also an address by a Dutch chap who had escaped to England when Holland was invaded. When, in fact, he told us that Montgomery knew that we would be facing two Divisions of German tanks but still sent us into Arnhem in 1944, he was not telling us anything we didn't already know. He was simply confirming it. What we did **not** know was that he – Monty – had neglected to tell our General of the presence of the tanks.

An Airborne Division is absolutely no match for an armoured division; it does not have the equipment to even give it a chance. But we faced not one but **two** SS Panzer Divisions, just so Montgomery could gather the praise and glory if we had succeeded. Anyway, after the inauguration ceremony there was a reception in the nearby Town Hall. Drinks and food were laid on, all free of charge. There was a very good pianist playing and after a while some members of the Dutch choir came in to join us from the church. A little lady from Liverpool organized a sing-song too, and it was great fun. General Sir John Hackett was present and when I asked him if he would give me his autograph on my picture, he said, 'I'll be pleased to sign your famous photograph'. A lady came up to me soon after and asked me for my autograph. She had Hackett's and General Urquhart's on the piece of paper she proffered. When I asked, 'Why do you want my name when they are far better-known?' she replied, 'Ah, but you're the only one who hitch-hiked to get here!' Fame at last!

That evening there was the second social gathering of the week. The first had been in a huge hall near Wolfheze but had been for British and Poles only. This one was in an even bigger hall on the other side of the Rhine at a place called 'Renkum' and included our Dutch hosts as well. There were more than 5,000 people under that roof. On stage traditional Dutch dances and songs were performed and in between times a very good jazz band played on another stage. Jimmy Edwards was in the hall and he played with the jazz band. He was in the RAF dropping supplies to us during the battle and was shot down but managed to land in Allied held territory, so he was there by right, obviously. My hosts, who had driven me there wanted to leave quite early so I told them that I would stay and try to get a lift back from someone else. This I managed to do having spent an exciting and rewarding evening with even more of my old comrades.

A parachute drop had been planned for Friday, 21 September 1984 at Ginkel Heath which had been one of the DZ's in 1944.

The day started windy and wet so it looked at first sight as if it might be called off. Soon, however, the sun came out and the wind dropped off, so that I was faced with the problem of getting there. The buses don't go out that far and my hosts were at work with their car, so they couldn't help. Standing at the crossroads in Oosterbeek I started chatting with the Liverpool woman who had organised the sing-song in the church. She told me that a number of British coaches were going out to the 'drop' and that there was sure to be room for me. Indeed there was and it was terrific. The atmosphere had to be experienced to be believed. Thousands, literally thousands of people turned out although it's about seven or eight miles from the town (this was the drawback to the operation in 1944). We were entertained by free-fall parachutists first of all and there followed the two RAF aircraft dropping 'two sticks' of our lads. I was watching the last man to fall, because he had his rigging lines twisted, but he recovered alright and landed amongst the crowd, the only one to do so. He was immediately surrounded by dozens of people, children mostly, who wouldn't let him go until he'd given his autograph to everyone who wanted it.

The drop was followed by a short service at the monument on Ginkel Heath and the crowd were very well behaved for this. Then everyone started seeking their transport for the return journey. I had been wearing my old red beret with it's distinctive 'RECCE' badge throughout these proceedings, by the way, and it seemed to excite a great deal of interest. People wanted to shake my hand, asking for my autograph again and generally making quite a fuss of me. I must say I loved every minute of it.

I spent the evening watching the Tattoo on the square in front of the Town Hall in Oosterbeek but the rain dampened the enthusiasm of many, including me, so I went back to my digs and spent the evening with my hosts helping them to improve their English.

'The Silent March' was held on Saturday, 22 September 1984 and was the principal event of that day. In the morning we assembled in the main square in Arnhem and with as many as possible wearing their red berets we were lined up six abreast by a regular RSM of the Parachute Regiment and marched off to the sound of a drum beat only. We were heading for the monument situated near the bridge that we fought for (the monument is the base of a pillar from the original 'Palace of Justice' destroyed during the battle – it is inscribed '1944'). This march was a silent tribute to those who died actually for and indeed on the Arnhem Bridge. The streets were lined with hundreds of Dutch people and though **we** were silent for the most part, the Dutch people clapped and cheered us every step of the way, a very emotional occasion.

There was a short service at this monument too, followed, once again, by another reception in a lovely old church nearby. Coffee and cake all round this time and I was pleased too, to meet two of my old chums from my unit. I spent the afternoon and later the evening, in the Schoonord Cafe on Oosterbeek crossroads talking to an English couple I had met outside on the main street. He was an ex-sailor but was fascinated by everything he had heard and read about Arnhem and came to Holland just to see everything that was taking place. They were very good company.

Sunday, 23 September 1984 was the really 'Big Day'. Everything that had occurred earlier was really a preliminary to this, the main service in the Airborne Cemetery in Oosterbeek. Prince Charles was to be there and Prince Claus of the Netherlands. Security was very strict. Passports had to be shown with tickets at least three times before one was finally allowed into the cemetery. My day was somewhat marred by the fact that I had an absolutely diabolical streaming cold and sore throat. But I was determined not to miss any of it. There were seats for most people but I elected to stand. Vera Lynn came by me and I shook her hand, Jimmy Edwards turned up too.

The service was very emotional, and was given by one of the surviving 'padres' from our Division and the lesson and service was delivered in both English and Dutch. A lump came into my throat when 'The Airborne Prayer' was recited and tears came into my eyes when we sang 'Abide with me'. At a given signal, hundreds of Dutch school children laid tributes of flowers on the grave of every soldier in that cemetery (I didn't realize it then, but this had been a tradition since 1946). Wreaths were laid on the 'Cross of Sacrifice' by the attending dignitaries and members of the units forming 1st Airborne Division. The 'Last Post' was sounded and the Association standards were dipped in salute. Raised again at 'Reveille' and dipped again on the playing of the national anthems (Dutch, English and Polish). A truly moving experience, one I will never forget.

The day was rounded off by a pleasant 'cruise' down the Neder Rijn on a large pleasure barge; drinks and a meal were provided and music too. This was a time to let all the emotion of the past week discharge and of course a chance for one last gathering before we all departed home.

I sat opposite General Urquhart and his wife and having excused myself asked him if he would kindly autograph my photograph. Without any hesitation he willingly did so and we exchanged some pleasantries – a true gentleman.

Monday, 24 September 1984 came all too soon, but I was anxious to get home to Betty. I said an emotional farewell to my hosts and as arranged my new friends – who had so generously offered me a lift home – duly arrived to collect me and my meagre belongings. We made one last pilgrimage to the Airborne Cemetery, so I could say a final goodbye to my comrades. The journey went by in a blur; we talked throughout, about my experience at Arnhem and as a prisoner. The crossing was uneventful and true to their word I was taken all the way home by this most generous of couples; I am in their debt.

As I walked down the gravel path, Betty was at the door. We simultaneously threw our arms around each other and seemed to hold on for an age; relief showed in her eyes that I had returned safely. Relief showed in mine that she was safe and well also. I think she also saw that the ghosts of forty years ago had begun to be laid to rest.

Chapter Two

Joining the Airborne Brotherhood

W e were well into 1944; I had been kicking my heels at Middleton Towers[1] since being returned as a non-battle casualty from Italy in December 1943, suffering with a severe bout of pneumonia. Regiments were being brought up to strength for the long-awaited invasion of Europe; consequently there were many postings.

On a personal level things were beginning to stagnate for me. The daily duties were becoming boring; but were suddenly enlivened when a notice went up on notice boards throughout the unit asking for volunteer wireless operators for the airborne squadron of the Reconnaissance Corps. Applications were to be made via the HQ Squadron Orderly Room and I was along there as fast as my little legs could carry me. Ken Hope and Pete Davies had been ahead of me and were making their exits as I went through the door. Events moved very quickly thereafter. Four Troopers and two corporals were told the next day that all arrangements had been made to expedite the move to Lincolnshire that afternoon. Ken, Pete and I were joined by Bill Cook and Corporals McGregor and Watson.

---

1. Middleton Towers Holiday Camp near Morecambe was opened on 19 August 1939 by Harry Kamiya. It was requisitioned by the War Office at the outbreak of war and used as a transit camp, Kamiya being interned as an enemy alien. Bought by Pontins after the war, it became derelict in the 1990s and is now the site of a retirement village.

An early lunch was laid on for us and we were told to parade outside the office at 1400 hours with full kit. A surprise awaited us! Our silly sergeant-major, late of the 11th Hussars had paraded the whole HQ Squadron and had the six of us lined up facing them.

Then, with legs astride, this stupid man, addressed the squadron bellowing at the top of his voice waving a hand in our direction. 'Now these men are soldiers, they are volunteering for an extremely dangerous unit'.

This was embarrassing enough but then he added to this huge faux pas by demanding three cheers from the assembled multitude. He then thankfully dismissed the squadron and came over to us. Quivering with embarrassment we wondered what his next move would be. He took Corporal McGregor's hand and shook it, and then coming along the line he shook the right hand of each of us. I was on the end of the line and it was only after he'd shook my hand that he stood and looked at us rather closely. 'Here wait a minute', he said 'you can't join the paratroops, you're afraid of heights!' My heart sank when I thought that this particular phobia of mine was about to rebound on me, but my Liverpool wit did not desert me in my hour of need. 'Well Sir,' I began, without a clue as to what I should say to the idiot, 'I've been making myself climb that ladder quite a lot and I've trained myself to live with it…the heights I mean!' It was all I could think of saying on the spur of the moment, but it sufficed. 'Good lad,' he said and it was obviously sincere, so sincere that I felt a pang of conscience for disliking him so much.

The night before, I had been to see my girlfriend Violet and had told her what I had done. She and her mother were furious, both saying that my despatch rider job was dangerous enough without sticking my neck out any further. So I wasn't really thinking straight when I said my goodbyes. That was my opportunity to have left my bicycle with them, but I was half way back to camp when I realized I should have done so.

There we were then on the point of departing and I had done nothing about my bike and I was pondering the point as we awaited the transport that would take us on the first leg of our fateful journey. At that moment, though, a friend of mine walked by. His name was Beechcroft and I stopped him and quickly made a deal with him. He would have the use of my bike until he was posted, but then he was to take it to Violet's home address and leave it there.

An excellent plan considering it was made on the spur of the moment, but with one large flaw, human frailty. It was only much later that I learned what had happened to my super bike. Beechcroft had got his marching orders, almost literally, but instead of following my instructions he had simply handed the bike over to someone else. This chap, or maybe an even later one, was riding the bike through Heysham one day and was seen by Violet's mother who was out shopping. She recognized the bike, so stopped the rider and told him in forthright manner that this machine belonged to her future son-in-law and that she was going to take it home. And she did – to the chagrin of the erstwhile rider. He must have been gobsmacked or the equivalent!

Meanwhile of course I knew nothing of these events as I was on my way to join one of the crack units of the British Army. We all treated our posting in our different ways, human nature being so varied, but I was tremendously excited. This might seem strange in view of the fact that I had already served in two theatres of war (North Africa and Italy) but the truth was that I did not feel that I had contributed very much to the war effort. Riding around on a motorbike day after day had become rather tedious and I wanted a change. This was initially why I had volunteered for the Wireless Ops course in the first place and now here I was knowing that the course had led to my latest move.

Our travel orders – in the hands of one of the NCOs – instructed us to go by rail to the town of Sleaford in Lincolnshire. We would be picked up by transport from our new unit and taken to our quarters. We had no idea where they were in fact but when the driver at Sleaford station saw us he quickly enlightened us. 'You must all be bloody crackers to volunteer for this place, from a place like Morecambe!' he told us. This was said without due regard or respect for the two stripes worn by our corporals. Watson bridled a little bit; McGregor just laughed and, conceding the point, replied, 'You could be right'.

Chapter Three

Ruskington

It was only a few miles further to our new billets in the village of Ruskington. A waterway in the form of a stream ran right through the centre of the village street and the lovely old church dominated the peaceful scene with its height.

We were quickly whisked into the presence of our new CO Major Freddie Gough. He was a career soldier we learned later, with three of his family having won Britain's highest gallantry award the Victoria Cross in previous conflicts. During his chat to us he informed us that the 1st Airborne Reconnaissance Squadron was largely parachute trained as well as being glider-borne and that it was up to us whether we completed a parachute course or not. On the financial side we were immediately granted another shilling a day for being glider-borne, but if and when we went successfully through a parachute course we would be paid a further shilling a day.

Major Gough impressed me enormously as a man who knew what he wanted and who would go to any lengths – legitimate or otherwise – to get it. The unit had been in action in North Africa and Italy and had earned high praise in both theatres of war from its commanding generals. After Major Gough had finished with us he ushered us out of his office, which was in a building which may have been the pre-war village school. A staff sergeant outside the office invited us to follow him and crossing the stream by a bridge we found ourselves outside the QM's stores.

Falling in or out didn't seem very important in our new unit and I noticed the Corporal, Watson, obviously disapproved of this fall in the standard of discipline. However or whatever, our visit to the stores meant that we all discarded our khaki berets and now donned the red beret, indicating to the entire world that we were now members of a prestigious airborne unit.

Almost opposite the QM's stores were two Nissen huts and we four Troopers were told by the Staff Sergeant to pick an empty bed in either one, park our kit on it, then come back to him for bedding. This we did within minutes and, with no further instructions as to what we should do, attempted, as British Tommies did, whatever the circumstances, to make ourselves at home. We were banging about the billet when the Squadron Sergeant Major came in. Jumping off our beds we expected a tirade of abuse from this formidable looking gentleman, but none was forthcoming. He introduced himself as Squadron Sergeant Major (SSM) Meadows. He then said that he would take us around the village and show us the places he thought we should know about. On leaving the billet we found that the two corporals were obviously awaiting us so we 'fell in' on them, making up two ranks of three men each. The SSM waved a hand saying, 'No, no! We don't do things like that in this unit!' And waving a hand again invited us to follow him. First stop was the mess hall, past the church and around a bend just a few minutes away from our billets. The two village pubs were next, which we saw only from the outside. Then SSM Meadows took us around the rest of the village, pointing out what he considered to be of interest to us. He also explained, during our perambulations, that no officer expected to be saluted every time he was seen in the village. One salute in the morning and one in the afternoon would suffice.

I was watching Watson while we were getting these rather controversial instructions and it was all too obvious that he did not approve. Corporal McGregor on the other hand obviously approved, as we did. We were all eager to get our first meal too. Not so much because we were hungry, but because we were anxious to see how well fed we would be in our new unit. The grub – we found to our immense delight – exceeded all expectations. Nor was it thrown onto the plate as in some places I had been stationed. The food was served with reverence and was made all the more appetising because of this.

The next day we all reported to the wireless wing and began to extend our training under the keen and watchful eye of Lieutenant Ladds. It was some time though before we learned his real name because everyone referred to him as 'Askey'. This was due to the obvious fact that our officer looked almost exactly like the popular comedian Arthur Askey with his short stature and glasses. Nevertheless he was well respected, particularly so because he knew his subject extremely well. There was nothing you could teach Lieutenant Ladds about the workings of an army wireless set. The sets, incidentally, were not the 19s to which we had become accustomed at Morecambe, they were No 22s. These though were only slightly different and we all soon became familiar with them.

Corporal McGregor had been promoted to lance-sergeant almost as soon as we arrived at the unit, much to the very obvious chagrin of Corporal Watson. Watson was now in the position of being the unit's senior corporal, having held that rank longer than any other corporal in the unit. This meant, in fact, that he was senior to men who had seen action in two theatres of war, while having seen none himself. He was a really unpleasant person and threw his weight and rank about in what seemed a deliberate effort to make himself unpopular.

This we all agreed was a stupid way to behave with men with whom he would soon go into action. About four or five weeks later a Second Lieutenant Pascal arrived and he too made himself unpopular by insisting on being saluted on every occasion. He did not seem to realize that he was the loser. Every salute he received had to be returned!

An unknown lance corporal arrived in the billet one day. He had come down from Catterick where he had been a wireless instructor.

Jim Stone proved to be a real character too and no mistake. For instance when a lance corporal is posted to another unit he is supposed to remove his stripe and start from scratch again. Not Jim! Oh no! He hung on to that bloody stripe for weeks, nay months after his arrival despite being told to remove it from his uniform. Ken Hope and I palled up with him and we became almost inseparable. Before long too, Jim, a good-looking chap, found himself a lady-friend in the village. She was a married woman, wife of an RAF Officer serving at nearby RAF Cranwell.

One night Jim invited two of us to meet his paramour in one of the pubs. Ken was otherwise engaged so I and a ginger-haired lad from Halifax went along. We assumed that Jim would simply introduce us and then we would be expected to make the right moves and depart. This was not the case however; we were invited to sit down at the table with this very attractive lady and she began to buy the drinks for us. She would not hear of our buying the drinks; she would give one of us the money and then when we returned to the table with the round, insist on us keeping the change. Together with Ken and Jim, I was to have many scrapes and adventures during our time at Ruskington.

On a more serious note, we began to be briefed for operations which might or might not be carried out following D-Day – the invasion of mainland Europe, which we all knew was not far away. On the other hand with time on our hands our beloved OC Major Gough was very good at handing out leave passes. He had made it clear that if a man was not otherwise engaged he might as well spend time with his family. As such on one occasion Ken and I accompanied Pete Davies to his home town and stayed with him and his widowed mother. However we were somewhat naughty (or rather stupid) in that we sewed onto our uniforms the wings of the paratrooper to which we were not yet entitled. On the return journey we were unlucky to be spotted by one of our sergeants also returning from leave.

So on Monday morning we found ourselves on a charge Army Form 252, for being improperly dressed. We went in before Major Gough separately and were both 'awarded' three days CB (confined to barracks). I took the opportunity to ask our CO to send me as soon as possible to do my jumps. He made a note of my request before I left the office. Looking back I still do not know why we were stupid enough to leave the wings in place when obviously we should have removed them before starting our return journey. But hindsight is a wonderful thing.

I had still not done my jumps when I learned that Ken, who was now in 'A' Troop, was with the other active troops, going down south to the aerodrome at Tarrant Rushton. It was now the end of May 1944, and we knew that the second front was imminent but had no knowledge of the exact date, nor indeed whether our division would be invited. Would the inexperienced 6th Airborne be committed to the assault or would the more experienced 1st Division take part? On the other hand maybe both divisions would be used, no one knew.

Anyway I was still in 'Reserve' Troop along with Pete and Jim so until or unless I was transferred to 'A', 'C', 'D' or 'HQ' Troop I was simply an interested bystander. The village seemed quite empty with the glider-borne men down at Tarrant Rushton.[1] The glider-borne element was down south at Tarrant Rushton and the Paras at Grantham. This was most noticeable when 'R' Troop went for meals in a virtually empty cookhouse.

A 3-ton lorry entered the village one day and I watched as the driver alighted and made his way to the orderly room. I went back to my billet. A few minutes later the driver came into the billet and asked for 'Trooper Evans'. 'Which one do you want?' I replied. Ray Evans was up at Barkston Heath near Grantham and 'Taffy'

---

1. There was no 'B' Troop at this juncture of the Squadron's History, it having been wiped out during operations in Italy and never reformed.

Evans was down at Tarrant Rushton. The driver fumbled with his paperwork and read out an army number…it was mine! 'What can I do for you?' I asked. Apparently there had been a tragic accident down at Tarrant Rushton, a Jeep had run away downhill, crushed a tent flat and gone over the head of a man lying down in that tent, killing him instantly. Now a replacement was required for 'C' Troop and I was it, so to speak.

I quickly packed my kit and in no time at all we were on our way down to Dorset. We arrived at a tented encampment which included the Orderly Sergeant, whose language was choice when I disturbed him to find out where I would be bedding down. Next morning I went looking for Ken and found him after breakfast as he and others were on the point of going up to the airfield in Jeeps to offload the gliders.

The gliders could only be left loaded for a certain period of time, after which they had to be unloaded and allowed to stand empty for a while, before re-loading could again commence. There was a wide side-loading door through which Jeeps and weapons could be manoeuvred and, in action, a detachable tail for ease of unloading. The tail of course had to remain intact until or unless the glider went into action, because it was a major job to put back together again if removed. Offloading therefore was no easy job and one that no one relished, but the powers that be ordered it to be done so we did it. Once back on the ground the Jeeps were driven off the airstrip to our camp where the contents, stores, ammo etc were checked over. We were 'standing by' and had been informed that we were to support the 6th Airborne Division when they went into France on D-Day, but only if we were needed, so we had no idea whether we were going or not.

During a check on the gear in the Jeeps an unpleasant fact emerged. Someone was pinching the fags and emergency ration chocolate. Other things were missing too, but mainly these two items were being plundered.

We knew without any doubt that the culprit was not one of our lads and subsequently two RAF airmen were caught leaving one of the gliders at night with their pockets full. The guilty pair received a summary good hiding on the spot; no further plundering took place.

6 June 1944 arrived and the massive assault in Normandy began. Our brother division, the 6th, and two American airborne divisions were involved, and after two or three days it was decided that we in the 1st Division were not needed.

So we began making preparations to return to Lincolnshire and as a driver I was detailed to drive a Jeep for the homeward journey. When we moved off, the sky was blue and clear but conditions rapidly changed and soon it was pouring down. The Jeeps were open vehicles without even a windscreen. This had been removed to facilitate the use of the Vickers K gun on the co-driver's side. It was customary therefore to wear a pair of anti-gas goggles while driving. I was driving immediately behind Ken at one stage of the journey. This was after a brief halt to stretch legs etc. As instructed we had applied hand brakes for the period we were stopped.

After a little while though, when belting along the road again, I saw flames coming from under Ken's Jeep and immediately realized what had happened. Ken had left his hand brake on! With the American Willys Jeep the hand brake did not operate on the wheels as with most vehicle; it worked by clamping onto the prop-shaft. This allowed the driver to move off simply by revving up a little more than normal, however the friction created generated a great deal of heat which burst into flame and smoke. I was honking my horn, shouting like a maniac and trying to overtake, but Ken simply thought I was racing him. He gave me the two fingers and made no effort to pull over. The Jeeps were capable of a speed of sixty mph and we were all near top speed on the otherwise deserted roads.

Eventually my mate realized that something was wrong and pulled over, allowing me to come alongside and tell him what the problem was. He blushed as red as his beret when the message got through to him. Thereafter, of course the hand brake was useless and the Jeep had to be left in gear when parked.

Northampton was on our route back to Ruskington and we had already been instructed to stop there for a break.

We rolled into town looking like nothing on earth. Gas goggles, when removed from our faces revealed clean patches around the eyes which showed the road grime on the rest of our faces. Slowing down to look for somewhere to park, we quickly realized that we were attracting a lot of attention but didn't at first know why. Parking on a piece of waste ground in broad daylight we became surrounded by people – mostly women – all bearing tea, biscuits, cakes and other sundry goodies. These good people began handing their gifts around and asking what was it like over there? Then of course it hit us! The worthy citizens of Northampton assumed that we were returning from the battles raging in Normandy and we in our own turn felt guilty about accepting this bounty. Our good Major though was not feeling at all guilty. 'Make the most of it!' he told us. 'You'll be earning it soon enough!' How right he was!

Chapter Four

Wings

S oon after our arrival back in Ruskington, I was informed that I'd be going up to Chesterfield in Derbyshire to do my jumps. I discovered too that I would be in the company of Sergeant McGregor and Trooper Bill Cook. For obvious reasons I greeted this news with mixed feelings, trepidation being high on the list. Jumping out of an aircraft is not the sort of activity one performs lightly and although I had been told that there was no disgrace in failure the one person I did not want to let down was me. There was also the humiliation of being caught and charged with having worn the Para wings illegally. This information became public knowledge in the unit and there were those amongst us who were not averse to making snide remarks about me not having the guts to complete the course.

With Sergeant Mac in charge of our documents a couple of days later we made the uneventful train journey to Chesterfield to whatever fate held in store for us. The driver of the truck that picked us up at the station had a macabre sense of humour. While we were loading our gear into the vehicle he began to regale us with tales about the monstrous events that had overtaken one poor individual or another. The one that stays in my mind, for reasons that will be obvious, was the very first trainee Para fatality involving a man named 'Evans', a member of the RASC. Driver Evans jumped with a chute which failed to open. This we soon learned was a 'Roman Candle'. Another incident with a chute he told us, involved a guardsman whose chute caught up on the tail plane of the aircraft. Well, bloody fools that we were, we wanted to know all the gory details. The pilot, obviously made aware of the situation, knew that if he landed with the man still hung up on the tail, the poor man would be scraped to his death on the tarmac. A daring suggestion from the Jump Master decided him: he'd make another circuit and while he did so the JM would clamber out along the fuselage and unhook the unfortunate man. Our driver had really got us now, although I must admit that I had begun to wonder if he was not exaggerating a tiny bit to put the wind up us! All three of us managed to exude an air of calm however, and the driver went on with his tale. Both the pilot and the JM knew that the odds against the damaged chute developing properly were very long, but it was the only option they had. The Guardsman had apparently fainted by the time that the JM reached him and had no idea what was happening to him. As it turned out, the chute did open after it was cleared from the tail plane and the unfortunate man made an acceptable landing, still in his faint. Our driver told us that when the guardsman was revived another chute was provided and the terrified man went up again immediately and jumped successfully.

He started on another yarn, but we had had enough, all three of us fully appreciating what he had been trying to do. Sergeant McGregor exercising his authority just said, 'right then, that's enough of that, let's go!' Then, with an afterthought added, 'by the way, I see you're not wearing wings!' The driver had no answer to this, but had the grace to blush as he climbed into the cab.

On arrival at Chesterfield we were driven to Hardwick Hall and were interviewed and asked about our attitude towards doing our jumps. All three of us were able to assure the officer that we were all volunteers, as were all potential Paras, but that we belonged to a unit that was Para and glider-borne. This meant that in the event of failure, for whatever reason, we would simply be sent back to the unit. Other aspiring Paras however – those waiting to join parachute battalions – were culled from almost every unit in the British Army.

These men on passing their course were then posted to one or other of the parachute battalions, either in 6th or 1st Airborne divisions. They differed from us in the sense that on failure they were posted back to their original units. RTU (Returned to Unit) was something we did not want to see on our papers. On a personal level, there was the very strong feeling of not wanting to let down our CO and our squadron while being aware of the increase in pay on passing the course. This, for me at any rate, was not the principal reason for wanting to pass. Hardwick Hall was now to be our home for a while.

Next morning was a real eye opener! Up at the crack of dawn it seemed, dressed in vest and shorts, the weather was not bad, at least it wasn't raining. Dear old Ruskington was a dim and distant dream from thereon and we were soon looking forward to being back there. Some way to go though before that happened. Everything was done at the double with one aspect outstandingly different from other military establishments. Whatever the instructors asked you to do, they also did themselves. No loud-mouthed bully boys here. Plenty of shouting admittedly, but all done with the best of intentions. No attempt was made to kill initiative; on the contrary it was encouraged. Paratroopers, we were told, had to learn to fight as a group or alone. The very nature of their going into battle meant that often a man would find himself entirely on his own.

The routine did not suit everyone. Three men in our group, before they had even been near a plane asked to be returned to unit. Their wish was granted without hesitation. One thing that was immediately obvious was that the quarters at Hardwick Hall had been constructed to house many more people than were there when I did my course.

Both of the airborne divisions were pretty well up to strength at that stage of the war and we three were really latecomers on the scene. Nevertheless nothing was skimped; we were not short-changed in any way. I'm sure of that because on our arrival back at Ruskington, when comparing notes with lads who had done their jumps earlier in the war we formed the opinion that we had had it tougher than them. Obviously with fewer men to deal with, the instructors could give us more personal attention. Strangely we took a rather perverse pride in that.

To give you some idea of why some men wondered why they had volunteered for parachute training, I recall a rather sadistic officer who insisted on us stuffing stones into otherwise empty ammo pouches before we started off on our pre-breakfast run. There was cliff climbing too, and descending using a rope without burning one's hands.

Altogether we spent two weeks at Hardwick Hall and although it had been a really tough fortnight we had every reason to be proud of having passed the tough physical tests we had been exposed to. Our next move was to Ringway Airport at Manchester where the RAF took us under their wings. We had expected that the only ones there would be the chaps from Hardwick, but we were made aware of the strangers in our midst when Sergeant McGregor was approached by a man who asked why he was wearing the red beret 'before' he had done his jumps. A brief explanation clarified the matter, but it made us aware that strangers were about – but we never did learn where they had come from or who they were.

We all hoped that the routine at Ringway would be less rigorous and, while the emphasis on keeping fit was maintained, we were not subjected to the violent lung-busting efforts we had had to make at Hardwick Hall. It did not require much intelligence to appreciate that all that puffing and panting during our two week stay there had been a test of character as much, if not more, than anything else. There was little or no emphasis on marching correctly; the main objective seemed to be to get the men between points A and B in the shortest time. Food was good, plenty of it. Best of all it was served by very pretty WAAFs.

At Ringway, the RAF parachute instructors began by teaching us how to jump safely from balloons and planes. This was done in a huge hangar with equipment in a rather bewildering array all around us. All this stuff was named the 'Kilkenny Circus' after a wing commander of that name. Earlier in the war old Whitley bombers had been used to take Paras to their objectives and this involved an exit – sometimes painfully we were told – through a hole in the floor. Now, however, the very reliable Dakota was in service and this meant a much cleaner exit through a door in the side of the aircraft. One piece of apparatus surprised us initially. It was like a slide in a kid's playground, but it was cut off halfway down. There was also a cable coming down from the roof, the use of which was quickly explained. A climb to the top was followed by throwing a toggle rope over the cable. You launched yourself into space and began the descent. At a command from the instructor you let go and went into a roll as previously taught. Both these devices were to help teach the correct way of landing when an actual parachute jump was made.

There was also an exercise nearer the real thing which was a device to give the learner a better idea of how to control his landing and involved donning a parachute harness and sliding down a wire. All of this had been evolved to help the would-be paratrooper control his descent and give him a better idea of what to expect when he did it for real. There were others too, gadgets I mean, but the use of them was all for one purpose.

We went from Ringway to Tatton Park in Cheshire to do our first jumps, which were from a captive balloon. These, we had been warned by many people, were the worst jumps of all because there was no slipstream to help develop the chute. Like stepping into an empty lift shaft is the only way I can describe it.

We stood around for a while after our arrival watching men making their descents from the basket below the balloon, with the NCOs on the ground bawling instructions to assist in a good landing. As far as I remember, each basket held four or five men, and of the ones I went up with for our very first jump, none, including me, could disguise their fear. On making my exit I closed my eyes, and feeling the canopy crack open was beyond words; but each time I asked myself, 'what the hell are you doing this for?' I never came up with an answer, but at no time did I ever consider quitting. After the two balloon jumps we went up in Dakotas and completed our course with four jumps in daylight, a night jump and a water jump. This was the most feared of all: the harness had to be taken off on the way down so that the chute didn't pull you under – but at least this jump was in daylight. If any Roman Candles occurred while we were there I didn't hear of them and I'm sure I would have done in the event.

My two colleagues, by the way, were recalled to the unit after they had done only four jumps. The unit had been briefed, with the Division, for an operation in Europe, and as they were members of active Troops they had to go back to Ruskington. Later the operation was called off but Major Gough deemed them to have done their course and they were allowed to wear their wings.

On my return to the village I fully anticipated being posted to one or other of the active Troops, but to my chagrin I was informed that I was still in Reserve Troop. A number of operations came up for which the unit was briefed, including, I remember, a drop on Brussels. The Allied Armies were moving so quickly though that Brussels was liberated before we could go. Altogether sixteen operations came up, so that when Market Garden was mooted we all naturally thought it would be another false alarm.

A few days went by though and there was no cancellation so it looked as if this would be the one. I was sitting in the billet when I heard a Jeep start up in the village street. I cannot explain what prompted me to look out of the door, but I did and saw our signals officer just about to get into the vehicle alongside the driver. Lieutenant Ladds was on the point of telling the driver to move off, when I on impulse, ran out of the hut and, after a hurried salute, said to the officer, 'Excuse me Sir, but if there are any vacancies, will you put me on the top of the list?' He nodded, signalled to the driver, and they left the village at a rate of knots, with me thinking, 'Well, I'll hear no more from him!' How wrong I was. The glider-borne troops of our unit were down at Tarrant Rushton again and the Para lads were standing by over at Barkston Heath near Grantham. Everything looked set to go. Security was very tight though and I certainly cannot remember being told, at that stage, what the objective was, nor our role in the operation.

Chapter Five

Lead Up to Operation Market Garden

W e were at Squadron HQ obtaining rations to take back to our country house billet outside of Ruskington. A chap emerged from the squadron office and came towards us. He asked if we knew a Trooper Evans up at the country house. When I told him that it was me he simply added, 'well don't bother going back there!' As I opened my mouth to question his authority – because he was a fellow Trooper – without further words he thrust at me the paper he was holding. The message was in effect a Movement Order instructing one Trooper D. F. Evans to move as soon as possible to Barkston Heath[1] where he would be taken on the strength of 'C Troop'. The lad had taken this message over the phone and had obtained the information that a Corporal Wally Verby had broken his leg playing football and now had to be replaced. Rather sensibly it was also decided I should be spared the long journey down to Tarrant Rushton, and instead go over to Grantham which was much nearer and join the parachute element of 'C Troop'.

Full of excitement I began running around like the proverbial headless chicken and of course had to go back to the country house billet to collect my kit. It was 16 September 1944. Would the Operation be called off or not? A vehicle was laid on to take me

---

1. 160 men of the 1st Airborne Recce Squadron would parachute into Arnhem on the
   17th September 1944 with 45 men accompanying the vehicles by Glider. Barkston
   Heath was the home of the United States 61st Troop Carrier Group equipped with
   C47 Skytrains or Dakota transport aircraft.

to Barkston Heath and when I arrived I expected to find a hive of activity and everyone buzzing with excitement. Not so. Men were going about their jobs as if the war was over, not at all as though the next day they'd be flying into battle. The sudden transition from calm to chaos was probably the greatest psychological barrier an airborne man had to overcome. A soldier on the ground in an infantry unit for example assimilated more or less gradually the sound and fury of battle, but men who wore the red beret, be they Para or glider-borne, were dropped literally right into the middle of it. So it was a pleasant surprise to see everyone conducting themselves in a calm and controlled fashion.

After the evening meal a few men in the billet started a card game of pontoon – a simple enough game with people playing against the banker. In my breast pocket I had three one pound notes and although I was totally opposed to any form of gambling, I decided to play. My intention actually was to get rid of the money before going into action. Beginners luck! At the end of the game I had won another three pounds so now I had six quid. A lot of money in those far off days, for a lowly Trooper. With no reason other than to keep the cash safe, I cut a slit in the inner waist lining of my battledress trousers and folding the notes lengthwise, slid them in.

All the other chaps in my unit who were to jump had been briefed about the operation but as a late comer I had no knowledge of what was expected of me. They soon put me right though! The operation was given the code-name 'Market-Garden' and involved three airborne divisions: the 101st and 82nd American, and the 1st British Airborne Division.

The plan was that all three divisions would be dropped at strategic points where they would capture bridges and hold them, allowing the British 2nd Army to charge up this corridor and enter Germany by the back door, so to speak.

The three main bridges were at Eindhoven, Nijmegen and Arnhem – all in Holland. There were lesser bridges too and all had to be taken to ensure success.

This was the brain child of our General Montgomery and many a British Para was to curse his name during and after the battle. Arnhem was over sixty miles behind enemy lines and the 'honour' of dropping there was bequeathed to the 1st Airborne Division. Opposition was supposed to be very light, with most of the enemy troops almost semi-invalids. Intelligence reports from 'reliable sources' regarding heavy enemy armour in the vicinity of Arnhem was ignored. This we learned later. The Intelligence Officer when presented this information – a Major Urquhart – was in effect told to shut up and was sent on sick leave. This too we heard of afterwards. The brief for the Recce Squadron was succinct: 'Get to the bridge and hold it!' This we were supposed to do until relieved, although apparently the bridge was only to hold for forty-eight hours, as by that time the 2nd Army would have joined up with us. One of the biggest problems, apart from having had only a week to prepare for such a complex operation, was that the whole Division could not be 'taken in' on one lift. With demands on our resources being made by the American divisions there were simply not enough planes and gliders to go around; although we did hear that General Browning had commandeered over thirty gliders just to take in his HQ. He was overall commander of Airborne Forces – what he wanted he got, despite this being such a critical point to the whole operation.

Of course there I am, a lowly Trooper in my billet taking in as much of the 'griff' as I could and also wondering how I would conduct myself in battle. Although I had seen service in two other theatres of war I had not actually faced the enemy, nor fired at him.

This basically was my reason for joining the Paras in the first place and I should add was the main reason for my not wearing medal ribbons in my new unit. It was not compulsory, so I never bothered. Many a young man that night, American and British, must have been asking himself questions pertaining to this situation. For some men – those Americans who had parachuted into France on D-Day – already had had their questions answered, one way or another. For many of us they remained unanswered at this point in the proceedings. Everyone seemed cheerful though; there was plenty of banter and leg pulling, none of it vindictive. At times like this you want as many friends as you can get; it's not the time to make enemies.

I tried to read once I'd got my kit sorted out. Some men were experimenting with the new bullet proof vests that had been issued and others with the bags that were strapped to legs for the initial descent. These held equipment that was needed on arrival in enemy held territory and were lowered on ropes on the way down so that the bags hit the ground first. The theory was that when this occurred, the paratrooper, relieved of the weight, descended at a slower rate. As we were to jump from 300 or 400 feet there was not much time to do this. The less time we had in the air – we were told – the less time that Gerry would have to shoot at us. Very cheering! Although I don't recall actually feeling afraid, when I tried to sleep at 'Lights Out', oblivion was denied me. I was not helped either by the fact that there was sound and movement in the billet all through the entire night. The toilet was probably visited more frequently that night than at any other time and there were men who would keep fiddling with their gear. For them I'm sure it was occupational therapy: unable to sleep, they just had to find something to do.

One man at least was snoring his head off; he was the envy of all those who heard him including me. Perhaps I should add too, that as I had been a member of 'C' Troop only briefly earlier in the year, I had not got to know any of them by name, so really I was going into action with strangers – not a happy thought! To occupy my mind I began going over recent events in my life. Violet of course was totally unaware of my impending fate, whatever it may be, and I began to wonder if we would have a future together. Then into my mind came the scene in the village church at Ruskington where a few of us had obtained permission to use the small hand-pumped organ. The vicar, a kind and understanding man had given us the go-ahead on the condition that we didn't sing any 'dirty songs'. My namesake Corporal 'Taffy' Evans played the instrument while one man pumped and the rest of us sang popular songs of the day. We were allowed to do this on the very firm understanding that the song we sang was a pure wholesome one. So keeping our collective word, not one ribald lyric passed our lips.

Back to the present, or at least to the current situation in my life. Dawn came and was greeted by some with relief and by others with misgivings. These were mostly men who had fought in North Africa, Sicily and Italy and were a real leavening of experience in the Division. They thought, though, that they had 'done their bit' as we used to say, and felt that another foray into enemy territory was tempting fate just a little too far. This I'm sure was largely due to the way that many felt the operation had been cobbled together. Originally when this operation was being planned, we, the 1st Airborne Division, were to be dropped as brigades in the main target areas, until someone realized that this would not give enough manpower at the objectives. The powers-that-be appreciated too that there were two American divisions standing idle, so the decision had been made, only a week earlier, to use them as well.

Again though I emphasize the whole scheme had been put together so quickly that only a week was given to organize the drop. Complicated as it was, this was not nearly enough time.

Montgomery however had prevailed over Eisenhower, the Supreme Commander, and all hoped that this single arrow-like thrust into enemy territory would mean that the war would be over by Christmas. There were political implications too. The Russians were intent on driving on into the heart of Germany and we, the British and Americans, wanted to occupy as much territory as possible before the Russians took it over. There was even hope that we could get to the German capital Berlin before the Russians did. By that time it was widely accepted by the western powers that countries conquered and occupied by the Russians would become satellites of the Communist Power.

So as can be imagined a great deal more depended on the outcome of this imminent Allied airborne invasion, than just the capture of bridges. None of this concerned us at the time though. Obliviously we were wrapped up in our concerns, worries and preparations for the forthcoming battle. There was no immediate urgency, on this fine Sunday morning.

Chapter Six

Departure for Arnhem:
Sunday, 17 September 1944

Conditions were perfect if they continued over Holland as they were over England, but there was no early take off planned. We were all due to arrive over the Dropping Zone (DZ) and Landing Zone (LZ) at about 14.30 in the afternoon. This meant that take-off for the glider-borne troops had to be earlier than ours as they would be travelling more slowly.

I recall the time of take-off was around 10.45am, fifteen minutes later than the glider-borne element which had taken off from Tarrant Rushton in Dorset. We were told our flight would last approximately three and a half hours. The planes towing the gliders were slower so the time difference allowed the air armada to rendezvous and arrive at the same time. I also remember an officer I think, coming around and handing out cups of tea laced with rum or brandy. Most of us drank it but I thought it tasted bloody awful, a waste of good tea or rum or brandy whichever way the individual saw it. We filed onto our plane at last, twenty to a plane. This was called a 'Stick'. With all our gear this was dangerously close to the aircraft's capacity; overloaded in the opinion of some. It was a beautiful day, as I had suggested earlier. Perfect flying weather in fact, so some of the imaginative wondered if the Luftwaffe would turn up to hamper our progress. The Allies now had an almost complete mastery of the air, but we knew that some German fighter planes were still about.

Take-off went without a hitch as far as we could see with our limited view of the proceedings from the small windows of the Dakota.

It was an almost physical impossibility, with all our gear on, to twist around and look out of the windows, but one or two wrestled themselves to their feet when we had stopped climbing and excitedly described the views that no one who was there will ever forget. As far as the eye could see there were planes and gliders all travelling on a dead straight course over the North Sea. Weaving in and out, up and down, were the fighters; there seemed to be hundreds of them. Down below we could see that the sea was dotted with rescue craft, emphasizing our control of the water as well as the air.

Somehow Sunday seemed to be a strange day for such a trip but most of us felt a great elation now that we were finally committed to an operation. This one would not abort now! We were all raring to go, superbly fit and full of the feeling that we were invincible. The enemy was on the run and we had been told that, if successful, this operation would end the war by Christmas. Many were going into action for the first time; little did any of us know how well these inexperienced lads would acquit themselves in the days to come. No matter how well a man is known to his comrades there is no way of knowing how he'll behave under fire.

Crossing the Dutch coast in perfect weather conditions our thoughts and reveries, sitting in the aircraft, were shattered as the German anti-aircraft fire opened up on us. The fighters dipped and dived, took them on and silenced them. Revelling in our complete superiority of the skies, again we felt that nothing could stop us now. The good weather continued all the way to the objective, the landing and dropping zones near the village of Wolfheze. 'Stand to the door,' seemed to come quickly, although the journey had in fact taken almost four hours. The dispatcher was standing by the open door.

The red light was on, changing so quickly, it seemed, to green. We shuffled towards the door, following the man immediately ahead, fiddling nervously with equipment, hoping that everything was in place and functioning correctly. No time to think now, we really were committed.

Leap into space, the ground seemed close; hold your breath while the static line pays out. The harness snaps around your body and you gasp with relief as that beautiful canopy opens above you. Very little wind, good! Pay out the line on your drop-bag strapped to your leg, it hits the ground, your descent slows and then your feet meet terra firma. Great! Piece of cake! No problems! Canopy collapses, hit the quick release, and join your mates as soon as possible. Everyone feels alone when making a jump. It's a strictly personal thing. Open the drop-bag, grab rifle, ammo – oh! Get this bloody over-smock off – always a damn nuisance. Now then where are we? Follow the crowd. Jeeps come into view, familiar faces with a variety of expressions. 'Come on', someone shouts, 'We've got to get to that fucking bridge'.

We joined our sections – mine was No 9, under Second Lieutenant Sam Bowles. Our driver was Bill Edmond, a likeable Scot. The Para battalions were forming up around us; they'd have to cover seven miles to the bridge on their flat feet. This, we all knew, was the biggest drawback to the operation; the element of surprise would be lost having to cover the distance between ourselves and the bridge at Arnhem. It would not require any great tactical genius on the enemy side to realize that the great bridge over the Neder Rijn was our target. The Recce Squadron brief was uncomplicated: 'Get to the bridge'.

So setting off on our various routes the Troops split up. 'C' Troop headed towards the railway crossing at Wolfheze station. Before crossing the line we turned left onto a track which was parallel with the railway. The first German we saw looked as if he was snoozing in the sun, sitting down against a fence post. The hole in his helmet, through which his blood still dripped, shattered the illusion. There was an ack–ack train of Bofors guns on the railway line that had been hammered by our fighters the day before; it was just so much scrap metal. We were startled when another German, who had been hiding in a ditch nearby, jumped up with his hands in the air. The Dutch Commando attached to our Troop, got hold of him, hustled him into the woods and simply shot him.

Within minutes of this happening firing broke out ahead of us and we heard the order for 'Dismounted Action'. Leaping off our Jeeps we sought cover. Most of the firing seemed to be coming from the woods at right angles to the track and immediately ahead of us and some of our lads were caught out in the open ground. At least two of our Jeeps were captured and the lads taken prisoner.

At this juncture I was still wearing my steel helmet and lying down facing the enemy. I was surprised to see our Medical Officer Captain Swinscow stand up waving the Red Cross Flag. There was a shot from somewhere on my right and he went down[1].

The weight of my helmet caused an ache in the back of my neck so I rested it for a while with the front of the helmet on the ground. As I looked up a bullet whizzed in front of my face, shattering a small twig near my left hand – I'd looked up just in time.

I couldn't make out where the shot had come from but assumed it was probably fired by the same man who had shot the MO. As

---

1. When this brief account of Des's part in the Sunday ambush was published by Robert Jackson in 1994, Robert Jackson wrote that Captain Swinscow was in fact hit by mortar fragments. However this is at odds with Swinscow's own account in John Fairley's *Remember Arnhem* in which Captain Swinscow specifically mentions surviving six successive mortar detonations, but then coming under machine gun fire, some of which hit the metal folding stretcher. Fragments of the stretcher or the ricochets then splintered off and wounded Swinscow in the back near his spinal cord.

the place was getting too hot for comfort I scrambled to my knees; he fired again and this shot hit the bandolier of ammo slung across my chest. Two close calls in as many minutes! (I managed to keep the two damaged rounds that had deflected the bullet until I was thoroughly searched as a PoW. The great loutish oaf of a German found them and confiscated them).

Hearing movement behind me, I turned to see members of the Glider Pilot Regiment who had been sent to relieve us. Those big chaps came up to me and asked casually, 'anything happening then?' I was quick to tell them that there was a sniper busy on our right and that he'd shot our MO. They didn't take very kindly to this and after a look round they headed across the railway to the opposite side. As soon as I saw where they were going I realized where the sniper was hiding and mentally kicked myself for not realizing sooner. There was a large bush beside the railway and as the pilots approached it a German emerged with a rather sickly smile on his face and his hands in the air. He did not smile for long however; three bayonets were thrust into his body and really wiped the smile of his face.

'C' Troop withdrew back to Wolfheze. Taking our wounded with us we placed them in the care of our wounded MO who despite his own wounds, started work right away.

A Dutch house had been taken over for the purpose with the enthusiastic consent of the lady who lived there[2]. Bill Edmond, my Jeep driver, had been killed during the action. I'll always remember him as a man who was extremely fond of his wife and was never reluctant to say so. He was buried in a temporary field grave opposite the house that held the wounded. Bill had died with one hand outstretched in order to save himself as he fell; rigor mortis had set in and this hand was sticking out of the blanket. A little later a Dutch

---

2. This was No 9 Deutskampsweg.

lady approached us with the suggestion that our dead be buried in her garden. We were pleased to do this, so Bill was disinterred and moved. Later I used his original field grave as a slit trench!

After we'd reorganized we tried another route to Arnhem. Evening was closing in so there was not much time before darkness descended. There was firing ahead of us and within minutes we came across a German car which had been riddled with bullets. The three occupants – a German General, his aide de camp and his driver – were sprawled in grotesque, unnatural positions, quite dead. They had been driving towards Arnhem, oblivious to the presence of so many British troops; men from the 3rd Battalion Parachute Regiment saw the car and just opened up on it. Soon after we overtook the now ruined car we saw 'A' Troop driving in the opposite direction. My pal Ken Hope saw me, shouted greetings, and with thumbs raised we passed out of sight of each other. Proceeding towards Oosterbeek we stopped for the night on the outskirts and were ordered to dig slit trenches. Lying down we tried to catch up on our sleep. A terrific racket nearby brought us all to our feet.

There was a large white house about 100 yards away and the exchange of fire was so intense that it lit up the immediate area. We looked to our Troop Commander Captain Hay to lead us towards the affray to help out our lads who were in the house. He did not appear to be as interested as the Troop Sergeant, Sergeant Christie, who formed two Jeep crews. Mounting up, we charged in like the cavalry with all guns blazing. Aware that a second pass was impossible, as we no longer had the element of surprise, we drove back to our slit trenches. (I have not yet found this house on my subsequent trips to Oosterbeek).

Chapter Seven

Monday, 18 September 1944

Next morning we were surprised to learn that we were returning to Wolfheze as this was in the opposite direction to the Arnhem Bridge. On arrival we went on patrol to cover the ground of the Sunday ambush. We were angered and horrified to find that the lads who had been captured had all been shot in the back. There was a suggestion later that this had happened when they tried to escape but as they were all lying in a neat row this is extremely unlikely. Another 'C' Troop sergeant had been killed here too, and his was a very sad loss. A finer man would be difficult to find. A Scot, Sergeant McGregor was kind, caring and always ready to listen and give advice if asked. Our dead comrades were buried in the garden of the friendly Dutch lady and all of us must have been thinking; 'There but for the grace of God go I'.

An officer approached me and asked if I had ever fired a PIAT (Projector Infantry Anti Tank). He was given an emphatic 'no' from me but unabashed he said, 'Act as loader to Cooke and then he'll fire it'. Jimmy Cooke had joined us from HQ Troop, probably as a reinforcement to replace our Sunday losses. The position for the loader was to lie alongside the weapon and slide a fresh projectile into the PIAT once it had been fired. A sergeant from the AFPU (Army Film and Photographic Unit) approached us and asked if I could strike a more dramatic pose. Picking up my rifle with bayonet fixed I knelt on one knee and said 'how's that?' The photographer smiled his approval using 'still' and 'cine' camera; he was busy for a few minutes and then bid us 'farewell'. This photograph, one of the few to come out of Arnhem, has been widely used in a number of publications about the battle. It graces the cover of John Fairley's book *Remember Arnhem*. Part of it is seen on the cover of Louis Hagen's book *Arnhem Lift* too.

There is also a large copy of it on a wall of the Hartenstein Museum in Oosterbeek. As the caption names only Jimmy Cooke I had been trying since 1984 to convince the curator that the chap in the background with the Bren gun was Trooper Fred Brawn. In 1987 I took the rather dramatic step of swearing on my boyhood Bible. 'I swear that is me and Fred on there!' This did the trick and our names were added to the photographic caption in 1990.

After the photographer had disappeared, Jimmy needed to answer a 'call of nature' behind a convenient tree. We heard the rumble of armour and down the road crawled an enemy tank. As the PIAT operator was temporarily inconvenienced, I had no option but to get behind the weapon. I took a steady aim, pulled the PIAT firmly into my shoulder (it was rumoured to be able to break a shoulder due to the large recoil effect of the spring) and released the trigger. The bomb flew straight and true and hit the tank squarely. It immediately stopped and smoke began to issue from it…no one got out! The tank was a 1940 vintage French type, commandeered and re-furbished by the Germans…a lucky shot!

In the afternoon we drove up the main Arnhem Road from Wolfheze and were just remarking on how quiet it was when there was a loud bang very close to us. Looking away to our right we saw an enemy mortar which had been firing on our troops elsewhere. It had been turned round and was now firing at us. The Troop Commander was all for getting out of it but I thought 'bugger this', and steadying my rifle against a tree. I tried a shot.

It was a long shot for a rifle, and the mortar was still firing at us. In fact we'd abandoned another of our precious Jeeps as a result of its

'R' Reserve Troop 1st Airlanding Reconnaissance Squadron, Ruskington, Lincolnshire, taken in July 1944 before the Evrecy (Caen) briefing – one of the many planned, then cancelled, operations involving 1st Airborne Division prior to Arnhem. Trooper Des Evans is standing, middle row, second from the right.

The famous photograph taken by Sergeant Mike Lewis AFPU, on the Deutskampfsweg, Wolfheze, 18 September 1944. In the foreground, Trooper Jimmy Cooke (HQ Troop) with P.I.A.T.; Trooper Des Evans (C Troop) kneeling with rifle and bayonet and back to camera; and in the background with Bren gun is Trooper Fred Brawn (C Troop). Trooper Brawn was killed in the ambush on the Amsterdamsweg on Tuesday, 19 September 1944.

The Grave of Trooper Bill Edmond of the 1st Airborne Reconnaissance Squadron, KIA 17 September 1944. Des used this original field grave as a temporary slit trench after Bill's body was reburied in the garden of No 9 Deutskampsweg at Wolfheze.

Studio portrait of Des Evans, taken in Liverpool in 1945 while he was on PoW leave.

Des Evans in an informal pose at Aberystwyth in 1952, whilst serving with a TA anti-aircraft regiment.

Des Evans on the historic DZ at Ginkel Heath in September 1984, wearing the original beret that he wore at Arnhem in 1944.

Des Evans and friends in 1986 at the scene where the now famous photograph was taken.

Des Evans in conversation with General Sir John Hackett, following the 'silent march to the Arnhem Bridge', September 1986.

Des Evans (centre) taking part in the Remembrance Sunday parade, Sherringham 1992.

The grave of Trooper Jimmy Salmon of the 1st Airborne Reconnaissance Squadron, KIA 19 September 1944. Trooper Salmon 'fatally' changed places on the jeep with Des immediately prior to the ambush.

The grave of Trooper Fred Brawn of the 1st Airborne Reconnaissance Squadron, KIA 19 September 1944. Fred is seen in the background of the famous photograph with the Bren gun.

The grave of Corporal Alan Baker of the 1st Airborne Reconnaissance Squadron, KIA 19 September 1944. He was fatally hit and fell from the speeding jeep, to be struck by a tree.

The last resting place of Trooper Bill Edmond of the 1st Airborne Reconnaissance Squadron, KIA 17 September 1944, in the Arnhem/ Oosterbeek war cemetery.

Des at the Hartenstein Hotel on his first return visit to Arnhem in 1984.

Des Evans (centre) wearing the beret he wore at Arnhem and in captivity, Remembrance Sunday parade, Sherringham 1992.

Vehicles of the Reconnaissance Squadron Living History Group parked at the actual site of the Amsterdamsweg ambush, during the sixtieth anniversary commemorations, 2004.

Members of the Norfolk Branch of the Parachute Regiment Association assemble to pay a last farewell to Des at his funeral in July 2010.

Mr Nick Clark, Standard Bearer for the Reconnaissance Squadron Old Comrades Association, standing in front of the wreath sent by the association. The wreath took the form of the unit's vehicle recognition sign: a square divided into green and yellow with '41' upon it.

accuracy. Raising the muzzle slightly, I fired. One of the mortar crew grabbed his chest and staggered back into the trees behind him.

I began running through the trees at the side of the road, my idea being to get close enough for another shot at the mortar crew. I became conscious that I was not alone, and still running, looked round. Five other lads had joined me. I remember Fred Brawn, Alan Baker and Jim Salmon, all from my Jeep crew, and I do not remember who the other two were. Drawing level with the mortar, without any discussion or plan we ran across the road towards it, shouting like lunatics 'Whoa Mohammed' – the famous battle cry of the 1st Airborne Division carried from its origins in distant North Africa. The two remaining members of the mortar crew looked rather uncertain as to what to do next, but this uncertainty was resolved when six more Germans came out of the woods to join them. I tripped, dropped my rifle and saw a bayonet coming at me; automatically I lashed out with my right hand and my thumb hit the blade. (I still bear the scar of this on my thumb today). My hand then came down swiftly to the fighting knife on my right leg (not the classic 'Fairburn Sykes', but a Bowie Knife I had bought myself prior to the operation) and I lunged upwards with it. There was a grunt and the German soldier almost collapsed on top of me. One enemy soldier was running back into the woods; the remainder lay at our feet.

Turning round I recovered my rifle and we started running back to the Troop. It was only later that we realized we had stupidly forgotten to put the mortar out of action permanently. Remounting the Jeeps we drove back to Wolfheze. (None of this was recorded in John Fairley's book *Remember Arnhem*, but no blame must be attached to the author, he wrote down only what he was told).

On arrival at Wolfheze I noticed a huge man in naval uniform; he was interrogating three German prisoners. The uniform looked incongruous amongst the army uniforms, but it was not that that attracted my attention. Every question was accompanied by a blow from a large fist to the head or body of a prisoner. A little later he took all three behind a house and shot them (I often find it strange when reading personal narratives that these more unpleasant aspects of war are never mentioned). I spent Monday night on guard duty beside a slit trench with a captured German MG42 Spandau machine gun for company.

Chapter Eight

Tuesday, 19 September 1944

On Tuesday morning the Troop Sergeant (Christie), being fed up with the Troop Commander's (Hay) lack of aggression, decided to take matters into his own hands. Two Jeep crews formed up and we drove up to a point near the main road. The rear Jeep halted while the front Jeep coasted up to the main road junction. On its return, having been pushed back so as not to make any noise, the sergeant told us what he had seen. We then pushed both Jeeps closer to the main road, started the engines and roared around the corner. A line of Germans were sitting at one side of the road having a meal; they never knew what hit them. With every gun blazing we sped past them and my lasting impression is of them all falling, like chorus girls in the ditch. We turned the Jeeps around and headed for Wolfheze.

Tuesday afternoon we were forming up to go on a full Troop patrol. Jim Salmon and I were detailed to go ahead as foot patrol. The crew of my Jeep at this point was Second Lieutenant Bowles, who was driving owing to the death of Bill Edmond in the Sunday ambush, Lance Corporal Alan Baker, manning the Vickers 'K' Gun, Trooper Fred Brawn, lying across the rear wicker pannier with his Bren gun, Trooper Jim Salmon on the right hand side of the Jeep, and me, Trooper Des Evans, on the left hand side of the Jeep. Jim and I were travelling with our legs hanging out board when riding. At this juncture, with the patrol about to move off, Sergeant Christie the Troop Sergeant jumped off his vehicle and jumped onto the back of the Troop Commander's Jeep. He thrust his Sten gun under Captain Hay's chin and said, 'If one of these men dies because of your fucking stupidity, I'll kill you my fucking self!' He rejoined his crew and we moved off. The paved road only ran a short way and then became three tracks running off straight ahead, to the left and to the right. The right one was our route and not far ahead was a large farmhouse.

As we approached it cautiously, a number of Germans, between thirty and forty, emerged with their hands in the air. The Troop Commander – suddenly feeling brave – ran to the front of the column and fired a Sten gun burst into the ground in front of the prisoners-to-be. There was absolutely no need for this as they were obviously surrendering. One of the enemy however took flight and made a run for it at right angles to our line of march. My reaction was automatic; my rifle came to my shoulder and I fired one round at him. He appeared to stumble and fall so I assumed I'd missed him but we found him later with a bullet in the head. I make no apologies for shooting an unarmed man. Had he escaped and obtained a fresh weapon in his hands, he'd have been killing my mates.

On coming up to the farmhouse we were shown a very badly wounded German. Both his legs were broken and both his arms too. There were other injuries – he was in a hell of a state. Out of the blue, it seemed, an officer wearing the khaki-coloured beret of the non-airborne Reconnaissance Corp came forward, took one look at the injured man and, putting a pistol to his head, pulled the trigger. Then in fluent German he began telling the prisoners to head back towards Wolfheze. It's strange, but I cannot recall having seen this officer prior to this incident, nor did I see him afterwards.[1]

Passing the farm we took a sharp left turn onto a rougher track that led through wooded country. Jim and I were still leading on foot. Proceeding with extreme caution the Troop began to make its way through this ideal ambush country. Then came the order to

---

1. Possibly a member of GHQ Liaison Regt – know as 'Phantom Recce'.

start 'Leapfrogging', with two men jumping off the Jeep that was then leading.

As I was on the left of our Jeep this meant that I was sitting on top of the '22' wireless set, which was 3 to 4 inches higher than the side of the Jeep. An excruciating pain made itself felt in my left foot, which was not helped by my jumping on and off the Jeep. Realizing that the other side of the vehicle was not as high, we were running back to the Jeep when I asked Jim if he would change places with me. He agreed to do so. This undoubtedly saved my life.

We were all mounted up when we saw the opening ahead where the track emerged onto a road. I cannot remember the 'Order of March' at this stage. But I am sure that our Jeep was NOT leading. I can recollect, quite clearly – because I was now facing that way – seeing a large number of Paras lying or sitting down in the woods to the right of our advance. Some of them waved and I waved back, so I assumed that they were just resting. Quite a long time later it did occur to me that they were all prisoners (probably captured when elements of 4th Para Brigade were attempting to withdraw into the Oosterbeek Perimeter), but I don't remember seeing any Germans. Possibly they had run for cover when they heard us approaching.

All finesse abandoned, we burst out of the woods onto the road and turned right – Amsterdamsweg. Looking ahead, I saw a tree trunk lying across the road and thought 'this is it – we're going to buy it now' – but no! We were able to drive past the left end or crown of the tree. By this time the Jeeps were going flat out; then there was another tree trunk ahead on the road and my thought was that this one would stop us and the enemy would pull the first tree across the road behind us. A clear mental picture of the Jeeps milling around while we were being shot to pieces, came to me.

However, again we drove around it. Then the firing started from our left. It was very intense and from well concealed prepared positions. I did not see one enemy soldier. There was no opportunity to see what was happening to the other vehicles. It was a case of every Jeep for itself. There is a vague recollection of one or two Jeeps overtaking us, but I cannot swear to that. I was trying to turn round to fire but it was out of the question. Fred's Bren was hammering away; I knew that Jim was firing but Alan Baker was firing the 'K' gun into the air, simply wasting ammo. I was then hit in my left arm!

As suddenly as it had begun – it seemed – it stopped. I realized that the Jeep was coasting and knew that the engine had been hit. Sam Bowles steered over to the right hand side of the road and pulled as close as possible to the trees. Alan Baker – already dead – fell sideways out of the Jeep and was hit full in the face by a tree. I'd lost my rifle somehow and had to jump off in order to avoid hitting the same tree with my legs. Fred looked as if he was asleep on the pannier and Jim was lying across the Jeep – his sightless eyes open to the sky. He had been riddled across the chest. I took all of this in at a glance.

I looked for a weapon and saw the Bren lying in front of the Jeep and was in the act of picking it up, when I saw that there was no magazine on it. Sam Bowles, by this time clearly wounded, was getting out of his seat and (it registered only later) was going the long way around the vehicle towards the trees. Calculating that there was about half a mag left on the 'K' gun I covered him by firing towards where I thought the enemy to be. It was while I was doing this that I was hit again.

A bullet came under the Jeep and lodged in my left leg. This was not bad enough to impair movement fortunately, because, following Bowles into the woods, I saw a wire fence ahead of me and cleared it easily. I gathered that Sam Bowles had jumped it too despite a wounded left foot.

I followed and caught him up just before we stepped out onto the road that led back to the 'Home for the Blind' at Wolfheze. With his right arm around my shoulder, both limping by now – he very badly

– we headed down the road.[2] There was a shot from our left after we had gone just a few yards. I heard the zip of the bullet before the sound of the shot, so it was close. I'll never know why there was only one shot fired at us; perhaps it was a German who realized we were wounded, but it may have been one of our own, who, having fired once, recognized us and did not fire again.

Arriving at the 'Home for the Blind' in Wolfheze we were greeted by a nurse who made much of us. Bustling about she quickly dressed our wounds and ushered us into an air-raid shelter in the grounds. We lay down on the straw matting covering the floor and she passed us two blankets each. By now, Sam Bowles was in a really bad way; his wounded foot was giving him a lot of pain and I noticed too, that his left hand was now also bandaged.

It is quite impossible for me to even guess at exactly how long we were in the shelter. There were bouts of intense pain and one day just seemed to merge into another. I have no doubt either that the good lady must have fed us, but I don't have any memory of what we ate or when. The nurse did apologize profusely for not having any pain killers and would stand there wringing her hands in her frustration.

It was during one of my lucid periods that the door of the shelter burst open and a tall Para stood there waving a .45 Automatic. 'Ah,

---

2. In John Fairley's book *Remember Arnhem* Lt. Sam Bowles is quoted as stating 'no-one came after me'. He may of course have been in shock and had not recalled how – with an injured foot – he had managed to navigate under his own steam to the 'Home for the Blind'. In 1994, during the 50th Commemoration, fate played its hand. Des waited to greet the coach party of 'RECCE' veterans. One gentleman who was obviously struggling with his case was none other than Lt. Sam Bowles. 'Let me help you,' said Des. The offer was readily accepted. As they walked side by side to his accommodation, he said to Des, 'Have we met before?' Des had his red beret on with RECCE badge; he replied, 'I'm the one whose shoulder you leaned on all the way to the Home for the Blind!' At that, Sam Bowles stopped and burst into tears, and admitted he'd blotted out the trauma of what had happened during that ambush in 1944.

she told me you two were here!' he said. Then he went on to explain that he was being pursued by a jerry patrol. Throwing him a blanket I said 'lie down and put that over you!' No sooner had he done this than the escape hatch at the other end of the shelter was kicked in. An aggressive looking enemy soldier peered at us and a smartly uniformed SS Officer carrying a Luger appeared in the doorway.

I was lying near the door, with Bowles further into the shelter, his wounded foot exposed, close to my head. The Para was lying on my left. The officer stepped between us and, holding the Luger three inches from my forehead, threw aside my blanket. Having ascertained that I was wounded and apparently unarmed, he glanced at Bowles, saw his bandaged foot sticking out of the blanket and turned away from me. I held my breath and relaxed my grip on my fighting knife which was under the straw. He went outside and his men moved away slowly towards the gate that led to the road outside the grounds.

I could hear their harsh, guttural voices getting further away – not then understanding any of their language. The Para stood up and threw his blanket back to me. I said, 'Where the hell are you going?' Even as I asked the question I knew what he was going to say. 'I'm going to give myself up – if they come back and find I'm not wounded they might shoot all of us'. Not being capable of physically restraining him, I argued, 'we'll take our chances – lie down again, put the blanket over you'. He would not be persuaded though. As he went through the door I asked his name. 'Joe May' he told me.

He walked out with his hands in the air; the Germans saw him; he went out of my sight. There was a lot of jabbering well within earshot, then a burst of Schmeisser fire. I felt sick in my stomach and my worst fears were confirmed when the nurse came in shortly afterwards and said, 'They've just shot your friend'. She was in tears and so was I. Hers were tears of sorrow while mine were tears of anger and frustration. Sam Bowles was totally unaware of this I believe. It is sad to recount what happened to this brave lad. He is now laid to rest amongst his airborne comrades at the Arnhem/Oosterbeek war cemetery. His full name was Maurice Langton May. He was 29 years old and his date of death is recorded as 21 September 1944.

On what must have been 22 September, three days after Sam Bowles and I first arrived wounded at the air-raid shelter, two Germans with a small van arrived to pick us up. Our captivity had begun![3]

---

3. Amongst Des's effects was a letter from fellow Arnhem veteran and author Ron Kent. The letter discussed the enigma surrounding the death of Pte Maurice 'Joe' May. Pte May had been a mortar man in Ron Kent's unit (21st Independent Parachute Company). Ron Kent confirmed that Joe May had gone missing on the night of the 20/21 September 1944. However he could not account for the reason why Joe would go west towards the encroaching German forces rather than south-east to the relative safety of the Airborne Perimeter forming at Oosterbeek. Darkness, disorientation, fatigue or pursuit by the enemy? According to the correspondence, Ron Kent had re-visited the battlefield in Oosterbeek in 1949. He was approached by a Dutch couple who said they had found the body of Pte May during the battle and had buried his remains in their garden. Their house was in the area of Ommershof (some two miles east of the Home for the Blind) which casts some doubt, around the claims made. However, Des had never read any account of the battle (having suppressed all thought); he had never returned to the battlefield up until 1984. How could anyone conjure up a name so distinct and yet which was merely a nickname and not the individual's actual forename(s)? One hypothesis that should be considered is the possibility that Joe May walking unwounded from the safety of the air-raid shelter with a pistol in hand had already been shot by the German patrol – this would account for the statement made by the Dutch nurse, 'They've just shot your friend.' Had he been shot dead, there is no doubt the German patrol would not have wasted time transporting a body two miles eastward, he would have been left where he had fallen. However having been shot, he may simply have been wounded and was then taken by the patrol in an easterly direction back towards Ommershof – but why then were the other wounded not taken away at the same time? Perhaps the wound was fatal and he succumbed to it by the time he was in the vicinity of Ommershof, perhaps he again tried to escape and was shot and killed (ironically Des himself had done the same to an escaping German prisoner on 19 September). Perhaps he was hit in further crossfire as a prisoner, or one must consider the possibility that he may have finally been the victim of an execution. It remains an enigma! 4039090 Pte Maurice Langton May, aged 29, Parachute Regiment, Army Air Corps, date of death recorded as 21 September 1944, now rests in grave 28 C8 Arnhem Oosterbeek war cemetery.

Chapter Nine

Arnhem Aftermath

My captivity began when I was picked up lying wounded in the air-raid shelter outside the Home for the Blind, Wolfheze, by two German soldiers with a small black van. They were not unkind in their handling of us and in fact were most considerate when they helped 2nd Lt. Bowles into the vehicle.

We were driven to a large house not far from Wolfheze. The Germans had taken it over as a local headquarters. If asked to find it now I would be at a complete loss as to its location.[1] Helped out of the van on our arrival, we were offered seats in the sun outside the house. There was a large Alsatian dog prowling around in our vicinity, but to my surprise it allowed me to stroke it. All enemy dogs – I'd thought – would be anti-British. A meal or snack was in progress and we were given a large thick slice of German bread with a generous spreading of jam. This was our first taste of 'black bread', as we came to know it, and though I ate it I did not enjoy it at all. There were many times in the next few months when I would have been extremely grateful for such generosity.

Bowles and I were taken that same day to the hospital at Utrecht. There is no memory at all as to how we were taken there. I have no doubt that we were driven to the hospital but I cannot recollect

---

1. It is possible the 'large house' was the Hotel Bildeberg at Wolfheze which had been used as Sepp Krafft's HQ prior to the battle. Taken over by elements of 1st Airborne Division at the beginning of the operation, it was largely destroyed in the subsequent fighting, but what remained could have reverted to its previous role.

whether it was by lorry or even by the small van we had travelled in earlier. The reception area was so busy that we had to step over stretchers lying about the entire floor space. Every stretcher held a body either dead or alive; we had no way of knowing which.

A young German soldier lying nearby was moaning piteously, with good reason – one of his legs was missing. Walking around was a tall SS Officer – possibly looking for men of his own unit who had been wounded in the battle? He stopped at the noisy soldier's stretcher and, looking down, snapped at him in German. The casualty quietened down immediately. When the SS man had gone, an English chap sitting close to us said that the young German had been ordered to 'keep quiet, as there were Englishmen who could hear him!' Our wounds were examined and we parted, Bowles presumably to an 'officers ward', whilst I was taken up two flights of stairs to an 'other ranks ward'. It was crowded! So full in fact that beds had been dispensed with, most of the men having been accommodated on mattresses on the floor. Some of the wounds were frightful. Arms and legs were missing from a number of the injured, but the overwhelming memory of that ward is the smell. In many cases the smell became stronger as one approached certain bed spaces. Gangrene was at work, and the lads who had contracted it in most cases knew it and were constantly calling out for attention before it was too late.

I learned that the surgery was busy day and night, with German and British surgeons working side by side. However, it appeared that the Germans considered that their own wounded were more important than ours. There was very little movement of British casualties down to the surgical theatre during the time I was there.

Security was however very lax. Sometimes there was an armed sentry outside the door, most of the time there was not. On a very bright sunny day, with another chap, I ventured out into the corridor. The route seemed to be clear so we kept going and, reaching the head of the stairs, descended one flight and then another, and eventually emerged into the open air.

Peering round a corner of the building we saw ahead of us the main gate unguarded, and wide open! With a studied nonchalance we strolled towards it.

Reaching the gate we took up a position to the left of it. There was a fruit shop immediately opposite with mouth-watering wares on display. There was a movement inside the shop, barely seen through the window. Then a pretty young Dutch girl emerged with two large bunches of grapes. Crossing the road she thrust them through the iron railings and said, without preamble, 'Take these. Do you want to escape?' Understandably the question took us by surprise, although the grapes did not. Thinking that the girl meant to help in our escape there and then, and considering the time and place to be quite wrong, we declined. Her disappointment showed on her face and leaving us eating the grapes greedily, she shrugged her shoulders and, crossing the road again, returned to the shop. It was only later, too late, that we learned that an escape route was from the rear windows of our ward. A ladder being brought across the unguarded area outside was, apparently, placed against the wall and escape was effected through another hospital building. Not knowing any of this when the brave girl put the question to us, we stood there eating our grapes then, turning, walked slowly back to the door from which we had emerged.

Reluctant to return to the confines of the ward with all its attendant smells and unpleasantness, we leaned against the wall enjoying the sun of the dying day. A very large open car drew up and a German General made preparations to alight from it. Almost insolently we gazed at this high ranking member of the 'master race'. Noticing our reaction (or rather lack of it), he turned red, then puce with anger, and started shouting at us in German, none of which we understood.

A young SS Officer, speaking excellent English said, 'Why do you not salute our General?' Before we could reply the General shouted again, still standing up in the car. Again the young officer spoke, this time saying, 'You should not be here without a guard – why are you not in the hospital ward?' Neither being panicked or overawed by the 'big-shot', so looking even more insolent I said, 'I didn't salute him because he's on the wrong bloody side!' I had realized that the first question was the General's, while the second question was to satisfy the SS man's curiosity. He rattled off some German to his superior, presumably telling him exactly what I had said, and was obviously amused by my reply. The General, however, was far from amused; perhaps he had no sense of humour. He went an even deeper colour and to the sound of his shouts we were ushered back up to our ward by armed guards. I learned later that it was no less a person than Field Marshal Model, and this was not the only occasion I was to see him, as the reader will learn.

The following day we had an unexpected visitor on our ward. A man walked in, dressed very smartly as a German SS officer. A major I recall. He surprised us by speaking in perfect English and then by telling us that he was a Dutchman. We learned from him that some of the enemy troops we'd been up against during the battle were, in fact, Dutchmen belonging to an SS unit. This was, at first, greeted with cries of disbelief, but he assured us that it was true. One of our chaps, a little bolder than the rest, then asked him, 'Well, what happens to you when the war is over?' It seemed almost without emotion that he replied, 'I'll be strung up from the nearest lamp-post!' His whole attitude betrayed his resignation to his fate. There were no thoughts of possible escape in his mind, not even when someone suggested that he leave the hospital and change into civvies. Bidding us all 'goodbye and good luck!' he turned on his immaculately booted heels and strode out to his fate.

Chapter Ten

Apeldoorn and Amersfoort

I have no recollection as to exactly how long I was in Utrecht hospital. Nor have I the remotest memory as to how I – with others – was transported to Apeldoorn. Although still wounded I was not taken to hospital there, which I learned in 1984 was at the 'Willem II Barracks', I was taken there for interrogation and pushed roughly into a cell. The entire complex in which I was incarcerated was on the ground floor. I can recall that there was a bed with mattress in the cell, bars on the outside of the solitary window, and a radiator. Before slamming the door, the guard informed me, in reasonable English, that opening the window would be regarded as an attempt to escape and I would be shot. With this happy message ringing in my ears, I lay down and tried to sleep. The cell was quite cool when I eventually dozed off. There were no bed clothes provided so I was lying down fully dressed. Darkness had descended when I awoke and it felt as if I were in an oven. The radiator was going full blast and I was reaching for the window catch when I remembered the guard's warning. Suddenly the light was switched on from outside the cell, the door slammed back on its hinges and a fresh guard beckoned for me to accompany him. He pushed me along the corridor using quite unnecessary force until he stepped in front of me, opened another door, and grabbing me by my wounded left arm sent me spinning into the room.

Seated alone at a table was a very smart German officer, not SS this time. He told me to sit and offered me a cigarette which I declined. 'You might as well have one', he said, 'They were dropped for you anyway!' This was a reference to the number of containers that many brave airmen died attempting to keep us supplied with during the battle. Most of them were dropped in the right places but by that time we had been pushed out of them by superior enemy forces.

He shrugged when I refused the proffered cigarette again and started to question me. Much of what he said was all absolute fact: time of take-off, name of airfield, name of commanding officer, height at which we flew and other elementary things. All he was asking me to do was to confirm it. I started saying my name, rank and number according to the Geneva Convention and as time passed he was becoming more and more exasperated, finally jumping up from his chair and threatening me with a raised fist. He seemed completely out of control but this may have been an act. The litany from me continued, name, rank and number, until he called out to the guard outside to take me back to my cell.

The cell was cool again when the door closed on me, so once more I tried to sleep. I was hungry too, not having been given any food since my arrival at Apeldoorn. Again I woke up at some unearthly hour with the sweat dripping off me. The same routine followed, on with the light, the door flung open, the rough handling by a different guard. And shown into another room with another German officer. This treatment continued for two weeks during which time I was fed on thin gruel and black bread. It was all contrived to break the spirit, but it didn't work with me. The monotony was broken on one day only: when being ordered out of my cell, instead of turning left as I'd always done before, I turned right. Ushered into the clinical atmosphere of a medical inspection room, I saw a young American pilot lying flat out on a surgical couch. I don't know why, but he had passed out.

The German orderly spoke to me in excellent English with an American accent. 'Bare your arm; I'm going to get that bullet out!' He then apologized in most sarcastic tones for the lack of anaesthetic.

Picking up a rather grubby scalpel, he proceeded to cut another opening in my arm close to the original wound.

There was no delicacy about the man. 'I'll make you scream you English bastard!' 'Oh no you fucking well won't, you German git!' This prompted him to jab more savagely at my arm and having made this hole he passed a piece of bandage through both wounds and commenced to saw it backwards and forwards. It was whilst he was doing this that the young pilot came round, sat up on the edge of the couch, saw what was happening and passed out again. He fell to the floor with a sickening thud. The German orderly ignored him totally; he was concentrating wholly on me. After a few minutes of this torture – for that's what it was – the orderly, disappointed with the negative reaction, snarled and with an angry gesture pulled the bandage from my arm, replaced the filthy dressing he'd taken off and almost kicked me out of the room. I was returned to my cell by a somewhat sympathetic guard. The bullet was still in my arm. No mention had been made of the wound in my leg and in view of the circumstances I considered it politic not to say anything about it.

A few days later, still wounded and now suffering periods of intense pain, I was moved with others – mostly airborne men – to Amersfoort. Here there was a holding compound for men awaiting transit into Germany. I can recall very clearly being, for the first time, thoroughly searched. A great loutish oaf was doing this job with obvious enjoyment. In front of him was a large table with a huge heap of confiscated English bank notes on its surface. The night before we took off for Arnhem, I had attempted to lose the three pounds in my possession by playing 'pontoon'. It was the first and only time that I had gambled at cards. Beginners luck! I ended up winning three pounds and this money was folded lengthways in the waist lining of my battledress trousers. He found it though. Stripped quite naked I stood before him as his experienced hands went over every inch of my clothing.

'Ah gelt!' he exclaimed with a huge grin on his stupid face, and added my six quid to the growing pile. Resenting the loss of my money, I resented even more the loss of two damaged bullets that had saved me from a sniper's bullet. I appealed to a German officer in the room but he just looked right through me as I tried to explain why I wanted to keep them. The bullets were tossed into a heap of miscellaneous items lying on the floor.

For some reason I cannot remember what Amersfoort looked like in daylight, but there is a lasting impression of a large square compound surrounded by barbed wire and the night sky lit up by searchlights. It must have been after a week had passed that, having been counted on a morning muster, some of us were told to get our possessions from the billets. We were being transferred to Germany. Many of us had harboured hopes that any day now the gates would come crashing down, smashed by an Allied tank. The impending move was bad news for us and even at the eleventh hour many men felt that the Allies could not be very far away.

Chapter Eleven

Destination Germany

I believe the train came to us, rather than us being marched to the train. There was certainly not much distance to cover before we were pushed – none too gently – into goods wagons of the type that were intended to hold eight horses or forty men. There were more than forty men in the one I boarded. More than fifty I believe. A bucket was supplied for toilet requirements, no food, and no water, nothing else. The door was slid shut. We heard the catch being fastened outside and found ourselves in almost total blackness. It took us some time to get accustomed to the darkness during which most of us tried to lay claim to space on the floor. When the slower ones realized what was happening and attempted to do the same, it quickly became obvious that there was not nearly enough room for us all to lie down at the same time.

Disputes began as to who was to have which space but were quickly resolved by a very large American who threatened to bang together the heads of any two who quarrelled over such an issue. 'We are there to fight the goddam Germans,' he averred, 'not each other'. Common sense prevailed and we worked out a rota system that allowed some of us to lie down at full stretch whilst the remainder exercised. There was no way we could know just how long we would be kept locked nor how long the journey was to last. It was vital that we travelled in as friendly an atmosphere as possible. With all the shunting and banging going on outside it became obvious that quite a long train of prisoners was being made up. Someone raised the question, 'have these trucks been marked with a red cross?' It was a moot point. No one knew nor had we any way of finding the answer.

The train remained stationary the best part of that day and into the night, then with dawn breaking a loud clanking and clanging of buffers heralded our departure. A couple of the more enterprising characters in our truck had by this time prised loose some of the slats from the ventilator, making it possible for us to see the countryside through which we were passing. Slowly at first then faster and faster we began our journey towards the 'Fatherland'.

There was a rending and splintering of wood as two Paras tore up some of the floorboards. 'Be easier to escape while we are still in Holland', one of them declared, and the other added, 'we'll go tonight, anyone who wants to follow us is welcome to do so, but give us ten minutes start!'

Every minute and every mile brought us nearer to Germany. It was a bright sunny day and we had occasional glimpses of German army units; lined up or moving along the roads.

One of these enemy columns seemed to be comprised almost totally of anti-aircraft guns and while we were passing it they were preparing to go into action. The object of their attention came roaring over the train! – an Allied fighter, judging by the sound and speed. Assuming that the column was the pilot's target we waited for the fireworks. The guns of the column were hammering out their deadly song when we heard above all the other sounds, the cannon of the fighter. They were aimed at the rear end of the train, not the German column, and we all instinctively crouched down awaiting the blast we regarded as inevitable.

The plane zoomed away before reaching our wagon, the 'ack–ack' ceased and the train came to a halt.

We later learned that there were a number of casualties in the four or five trucks at the end of the train but mercifully we were spared. The irony of situation hadn't escaped us. We, Allied soldiers had been saved by the enemy 'ack-ack' column on the road. We also knew that the question asked previously had been answered; the trucks were <u>not</u> marked with the Red Cross.

That night the two Paras awaited their opportunity, and feeling the train slow down, dropped one after the other into the unknown. They were followed a little later by two or three more. I have never learned of their fate and do frequently wonder what happened to them. Each wagon had a guard sitting on the roof facing the direction of the train, but we heard no firing and assumed that they got clean away.

The following day we were strafed again and further casualties occurred. Fortunately that was the last time this happened. Somewhere along the way we crossed the German frontier. We stopped and the door was opened to allow us to get out to refresh ourselves, empty the bucket and receive a small piece of black bread and an even smaller piece of sausage. Water was provided in a clean bucket, enough for drinking but not for washing ourselves. Here too German nurses came along the platform asking if any wounded wanted fresh dressings applied to their injuries. I took off my BD blouse, rolled up my sleeve and waited until a nurse was free to attend to me. A large beefy female grabbed my arm, roughly removed the cloth bandage and even more roughly applied a paper bandage, binding it around my arm far too tightly.

Discomfort wasn't immediately apparent but later it became really painful and when I showed it to an American medical orderly he told me quite bluntly that if I didn't take it off I'd lose my arm. This was two or three days later, when we were well into Germany. Without hesitation I ripped it off. The relief was enormous. My arm, near my left elbow, was so reduced in size that I was able to circle it with the finger and thumb of my other hand. No bandages being available I pulled down my sleeve and hoped that my wound would remain uninfected by the now filthy conditions in the railway wagon.

With the best will in the world I must conclude that the German nurse's ministrations were performed with a view to deliberately causing me as much discomfort as possible. I can still see her big red face contorted with the effort of putting the paper on as tightly as possible. No doubt she went home later satisfied she had 'done her bit' for the war effort.

Each day there was a halt and each day we were given black bread and sausage and on more than one occasion some hot soup as well. This was of doubtful vintage and origin. No one dared suggest what was in it, but we hoped it was nourishing, which was enough to warrant the consuming of every drop. Each day too, during these stops, we realized that our train was being split, and presumed – correctly as it turned out – that the wagon loads of prisoners were being sent to various parts of Germany and Poland.

One night we halted in a large railway complex and an American chap said that we were in Cologne. He spoke German and had overheard the guards talking before they were relieved. Removal of the loose slats enabled us to look out into the darkness but we could see nothing to prove or disprove what the German speaking American had said. Then the sound we all dreaded rent the night, the sirens wailed their awful message. We were hclpless, locked inside a goods wagon on a railway line in the centre of Cologne, one of the most bombed cities in Hitler's Reich! This gave the lie to Goering's boast that no Allied bombers would be allowed to attack any German city.

Searchlights began flinging their white fingers across the sky and 'ack-ack' guns opened up in the haphazard hope of hitting a bomber. Bombs began to fall and we were practically fighting to get a view through the limited space offered by the broken ventilator. A young chap, red haired and a member of the Border Regiment, began to show signs of extreme agitation. Clenching and unclenching his fists he was moaning and muttering unintelligible words rising in volume and pitch as the noise outside grew louder. There was a thud on the platform outside the wagon and we knew that a bomb had landed very close to us. We waited for the explosion that we all felt would take us to meet our 'Maker'. Hour after hour we sat or stood not knowing if the bomb was delayed action or, we prayed, a dud. The lad from the Borders was driven over the edge by waiting. Jumping to his feet from his place on the floor in the corner of the truck, he started clawing at the door, ripping off his fingernails and reducing his fingers to bloody shreds. He was restrained by two of the biggest men in our company; they had to sit on him to prevent further damage to himself.

It was the longest night of my life and I'm sure many of the others felt the same way. Eventually dawn came and we were able to see some of the devastation caused by the air raid. Cologne Cathedral stood out stark against the surrounding ruins. Of more concern to us was the large hole within six feet of our wagon. Any time now it might reach the end of its delayed fuse and our journey into the Third Reich would be over. It was with profound relief that we heard the whistle of an engine and felt ourselves being shunted away from that place. We blessed the faulty workmanship that had determined that this particular bomb had not exploded – at least while we were there!

One day succeeded another. To me and others it gave the impression that the journey was almost endless. It seemed that way because it is impossible to say how long we were locked in that dreadful wagon. Imagination and rumour ran riot; we had no idea as to our ultimate destination or fate. Attempts to gain information from our guards during daily halts were greeted with rough handling or a stony silence. The German-speaking American quite sensibly thought that it would be better if the enemy did not know of his linguistic ability. That way he might gain intelligence as to what was happening to us from talkative guards outside the wagon. We paratroopers were all aware of Hitler's edict that all 'terror' troops, including commandos and airborne soldiers, should be shot. At least we had some consolation from the fact that it hadn't happened thus far.

It would seem pointless, we told ourselves, to transport us all the way into Germany just to shoot us. We were not then fully aware of the enormity of Hitler's destruction of the Jewish race and their having been transported hundreds of miles to expedite their deaths. This would have been small comfort to us had we known.

Chapter Twelve

Journey's End; Frankfurt-Am-Main

Journey's end came for us in a large goods siding. It was part of a much bigger marshalling yard which covered many acres. The door slid open minutes after we had halted and a very amiable guard invited us to jump down. Ours was the only truck to reach this destination; the others were still heading for, or had reached, their off-loading points. Railway lines seemed to stretch as far as the eye could see in all directions giving rise to the thought that there was another marvellous target for the Allied bombers. There was some damage but from our ground level viewpoint it was quite impossible to fully estimate it. Between tracks we were formed up into a column and given orders in broken English, to march towards what transpired to be the main station of a large city. With memories in our minds of the removal of all railway name boards in England during the time when we were expecting invasion, it was with some surprise that we saw letters indicating with absolute certainty that we had arrived in Frankfurt-am-Main.

The column was marched up the sloping end of the platform and we found ourselves almost mingling with the passengers, both civilian and military. This was cause for not a little uneasiness in our ranks; we had no idea how the German man in the street felt about us. The thought that we were to be involved in a display of anti-Allied feeling was engendered when a middle-aged man in a smart suit stepped out of the crowd and spat at us. He stood his ground and sneered at us and treated us to what we could only assume was a stream of verbal abuse and invective. The friendly German NCO snapped an order to a guard in the rear and the guard responded by driving the butt of his rifle into the angry civilian's mouth. He fell back astonished, spitting out teeth.

Many of us felt that this was an extreme measure but later realized that the NCO was putting out the fire before it could develop into a larger conflagration. It may have required very little incentive to turn the hundreds of people in the station into a massive pack of baying hounds after our blood. It was after some time in German hands, that I learned that the Germans who had the least regard for one's comfort and safety were those who had not been directly involved in the conflict.

After this incident most of the covert glances in our direction were purely to assuage the curiosity of the onlooker. Nothing more untoward happened until a passenger train pulled into the platform on which we stood. Then the mass of people surged forward with the obvious intention of boarding it. There were shouts from our guards and, wielding rifle butts like flails, they drove back the would-be passengers. There was utter confusion, the people not understanding this assault on their persons any more than we did. The NCO started to harangue the crowd, some of them nursing bruises and still more of them looking as though they would murder us on the spot. Translated by our American friend in undertones, the German was telling his compatriots that we were soldiers who had fought a great battle and therefore must be treated with respect. Part of the train – he went on – had been allocated to us and we must be allowed to board first.

By British standards – even war time standards – the train, or at least the compartments into which we were ushered, were spartan. The hard un-cushioned seats however were sheer bliss after our most recent mode of travel and we sat down with sighs of relief.

Guards patrolled the corridor and kept an eye on the civilian passengers who were now allowed to board the remainder of the train. There was an altercation, albeit brief, when a passenger attempted to push his way through our carriage via the corridor to the coach ahead of ours. Very disgruntled he alighted and made his way to the other coach by way of the platform, glaring at us as he went by. One brave son – some thought foolhardy – put up two derisive fingers and grinned all over his face. It was quite evident by the expression on the German civilian's face that he felt that having been defeated we should now lie down. The show of sheer defiance certainly puzzled him.

There was a half hour delay during which the NCO came along the corridor to apologize, to the obvious chagrin of some of his men. To apologize to the captured enemy was totally unnecessary they obviously thought, but to apologize because the super efficient *Eisenbahn* was tardy was unthinkable. It was not done in a deprecating manner though, he was fully aware that we had had a long and uncomfortable and traumatic journey and were looking forward to a place where we could lay our weary heads. In retrospect it is difficult to understand why he did not tell us that we were facing only a short journey. Short journey it was, lasting only thirty-five minutes.

The train pulled into a station proclaiming it to be Weimar; I cannot recollect clearly what the correct spelling was. Fortunately the weather was kind. It was a lovely sunny autumn day. None of us were equipped or dressed for wet weather. It seemed strange and somewhat incongruous to be passing through the turnstile without being asked for a ticket. Judging by the look on the station master's face, he at least thought we ought to be paying for the privilege of travelling on 'his' railway.

Marshalled outside the station, on the dusty road, we were counted, as far as I know, for the second time and then directed to march off with the guards leading and around us. A village or small town was ahead on our route and as we trudged through, the populace turned out to line our route. Expecting some sort of reaction we were all taken aback to be greeted by complete silence. They just stood there, having turned out to witness our passing, with not a word, not a single solitary syllable. It was most disconcerting.

The PoW camp came into view. We were not weary from our march; the camp was possibly two or three miles from the station. We were weary from the lack of sleep, lack of exercise and fresh air and some – like myself – had suffered and were still suffering from their wounds. The camp was divided by the road on which we marched, with the prisoners' quarters on our right and the administration buildings on the left. A small gate was opened from inside by the guard and we began to enter the prison camp proper for the first time.

Then there occurred one of the most puzzling episodes of my whole life. The gate was wide enough to pass through in single file only. Standing just inside were two RAF men looking as if they were filling time on a sunny day watching these new prisoners enter the camp. As I drew level with them, I was amazed when they seized me – none too gently – by an arm each. I struggled and tried to tell the man on my left that I still had a bullet in that arm. To no avail however, whatever thy planned to do they were going to do it anyway. 'You're RECCE Squadron, aren't you?' one of them asked.

Wearing my red beret with its distinctive badge of the 1st Airborne Reconnaissance Squadron should have left them in no doubt, but I nodded and said, 'What's all this about?' Heading towards one of the nearby wooden buildings I was asked to be patient and they now held me less forcibly. Inside the building, which was part of the sleeping accommodation, I was steered towards the large window which overlooked the open space we had recently crossed. A British soldier came into sight walking slowly past the window. 'Look at that man! Do you know him?' I was asked. Had the window been opened I could have called out because I recognized him immediately. 'Do you know him?' I was asked again. 'Yes I do, it's a chap named Vaughn from my unit!' I told them. Still mystified at this cloak and dagger business I said, 'to hell with you. I'm going outside to speak to him!' 'Don't do that until you see what happens!' said one of them. My curiosity aroused, I waited and watched. Vaughn continued his leisurely stroll and appeared to be heading for the gate through which I had so recently passed. He spoke to the guard who, without hesitation, unlocked the gate allowing Vaughn to pass through, continuing across the road dividing the camp; he spoke to the German at the second gate. This guard too unlocked his gate and Vaughn walked through and into the admin building.

'Now I'm really puzzled' I exclaimed. 'What's he up to?' Inviting me to sit down, the two RAF lads looked at me very intently for a few seconds, then one asked, 'How well do you know him; did you know he spoke perfect German and are you sure it's who you think it is, this chap Vaughn?' Already I had realized that this was a serious matter and that my help was needed. I told them that I'd been out to local hostelries back in England with Vaughn. The fact that he spoke German at all amazed me. I'd had no idea that he had any talent for foreign languages. There was no doubt at all in my mind either, that it was Trooper Vaughn.

It seemed that they had thought him to be a 'ringer' – a German or a member of an allied country – allied to Germany that is – who had been placed in camp as a spy. Being on the inside, he could then inform on any prisoners who were planning escapes, who had radios, traded with the guards or any other data that might be of interest to the Camp Commandant. If this WAS the case then why was Vaughn doing it all so openly?

Now I should explain that this camp – Oberursel – up to our arrival was exclusively for RAF personnel; flying crew who had been shot down over Germany. The reason for our being there was that German paratroops were part of their Air Force and so the Germans were treating us in the same way. One must feel, however, that at that stage of the war, with their usual Teutonic efficiency, the enemy should have known that British Paras formed part of the army.

It was a very well organized camp. Red Cross parcels were available, but when issued to the individual, cigarettes, chocolates and similar items were given to him, but all food stuffs were taken to the kitchen where they were pooled. There was a large, clean, airy dining room where food was dished out on plates, very much like military messes back home. It was not even necessary to wash one's plates after the meal, this duty being performed by men who were detailed for the job.

There was no shortage of volunteers; it seemed, with extra food for the dishwashers it was regarded as a sinecure. It helped to pass the time too, the importance of which was not yet apparent to us new 'Kriegies' (*Kriegsgefangeners*) or prisoners. Our stay there was short. After three or four days the Germans realized they'd made a mistake and told us that we were being moved. During my stay I never saw Vaughn again. I cannot imagine why because it was such a small camp. Perhaps he was spirited away!

There was however an interesting sequel to this part of my story. Years later, when I lived in Gloucestershire, I was sent to Lincoln from my place of work to deliver some pamphlets to an exhibition site. As this meant a night away from home, to me it seemed logical that I should spend the night in Ruskington. This was the village in which we were stationed before going to Arnhem in 1944. Driving the 16 or 17 miles to the village, I enquired at the local pub as to whether they could provide bed and breakfast. The landlord said that he could provide the bed, in a caravan, but not the breakfast. Thinking that an explanation might further my cause, I gave him my reason for wanting to stay there. 'Oh!' he said, 'I see, we have one of your old unit living in the village now.' When I asked if he knew the man's name he said that it was 'Vaughn' and that he had returned to marry the girl he'd got in the family way. This rang a distant bell; I remembered that my erstwhile comrade had told me one night in his cups, that his girlfriend was pregnant. I have since been back to reunions at Ruskington but there was no sign of Trooper Vaughn. I eventually ended up spending the night in Sleaford a small town four miles from Ruskington.

Chapter Thirteen

Stalag XIIA Limburg

All paratroopers in the camp, British and American, were moved out the following day. Once again I must plead a failed memory. I have no recollection of how we were transported to our next Stalag. This turned out to be XIIA at Limburg[1]. What a dump! There was absolutely no comparison with the conditions we had left behind. It was raining heavily when we turned up outside the gates. We were not expected and were kept waiting in the downpour whilst the commandant made up his mind as to whether he would accept us or not. An hour and a half later, almost reluctantly it seemed, the gates were opened and we had to go through the routine of being registered. Each man was issued with a PoW tag, a piece of metal about 2½ inches by 2 inches with perforations running across it lengthways. The man's number was stamped on both sides of the perforation so that in the event of his death one half would be broken off and the other half left with the body. My PoW number was 92799; this I can remember because I still have the whole tag.

Stalag XIIA was crowded. It was so full that huge marquees had been erected to accommodate the overflow. Inside the more permanent buildings, bunk beds were provided three high, but in the marquees loose straw, not very clean, was spread on the ground. As late arrivals, we were allocated spaces in one of the tents. To

---

1. Stalag XIIA was at Limburg in the state of Hesse.

say that conditions were primitive would be putting it mildly. The toilets were mere holes in the ground with very little privacy and there was one fresh water tap, on a post outside, for hundreds of men. So keen was I to keep myself clean that at the first opportunity I stripped off and standing by the tap gave myself an all-over wash. This was greeted by shouts of derision from some of the other PoWs but others were honest enough to say that they wished they'd had the guts to follow my example. Later some of them did so, waiting by the tap for me to turn up and strip off first. Getting clean in this way was a real hardship initially, but later when winter arrived with a vengeance, one of the worst winters in recorded history, it was hardship indeed.

Many of the men were stricken with dysentery and there was the sound of running feet all through these winter nights. It was necessary to call out to the German guard on patrol before emerging from the tent, otherwise there was a very real danger of being shot. There were mishaps, many of them, when men did not jump up quickly enough to get to the toilets. These poor souls were easily spotted in the light of day by the fact that everyone else was giving them a wide berth. It was far too cold to take off their soiled clothing for washing and there were no spares to replace the filthy garments they were wearing. I was fortunate; it was not to be my lot to be similarly stricken, but my heart went out to these men, American and British. Their condition must have driven them to the depths of soul-destroying misery.

In such a crowded camp the queue to see the doctor was, predictably, very long. Every morning the British medical staff tried to cope with the ever increasing number of men who reported sick. Resources were extremely limited. All pleas to the Germans were met with polite refusals or the excuse that most medical supplies were needed at the front. The MO was in despair. A conscientious man, he could see he was losing the battle when every day two or three corpses were carried out of the camp for burial.

I was brought down with influenza and admitted to the camp hospital and whilst lying in bed realized that I had small foreign bodies crawling about my person. They were bed bugs and they were hungry, persistent little buggers. The motto, I remembered at the time, was 'don't scratch em, catch em'! This we endeavoured to do, because we in the hospital ward all had them. They were having a field day, and night! During my sojourn in the hospital a paratrooper officer was brought in for treatment. His mouth was bloody and most of his front teeth were missing. The general opinion, at first, was that he'd been involved in a fight with another PoW. This however was not the case. It seems that a German guard took it upon himself to exercise his authority. He ordered the officer to fill a bucket with water, supplied him with a scrubbing brush, then pushing the Para outside had ordered him to start scrubbing the dirt road running through the camp. The officer, already at a low ebb from the conditions, lack of food and dreadful cold, tried to protest. Without warning the guard drove the butt of his rifle into the man's mouth. When the story got around – as it quickly did – feelings ran very high throughout the camp. The German commandant assured us that the offending guard would be disciplined but nothing more was heard of the matter. The guard was, at least, posted away; he was not seen in the camp again.

Limburg was bombed two or three times whilst I was in the camp. The town of Limburg which was quite close to us, uncomfortably close we felt when the bombers were overhead, had incurred quite a lot of damage. Word went round, first thought to be a rumour, that volunteers were required to go into the town and clear up the mess. Soon, it was made official, and parties were leaving camp every day on the understanding that their rations would be increased to supply the energy needed for the work. I was in the hospital when this news filtered through to us, so was in no position to volunteer.

There was a longing to do something, anything to break the appalling monotony. My influenza attack had been defeated but before leaving the hospital the MO said that he would look at my wounds. Apart from the occasional twinge, I had almost forgotten them. The doctor rolled up my left sleeve and there sitting very near the surface was a bullet. With a pair of tweezers it was very gently plucked out. The bandage on my leg was unwound and a similar thing had happened there too. My body had finally rejected the objects that had given me so much pain and discomfort.

Discharged from the hospital that day, I again took up residence in a marquee. The weather was bitterly cold and many of the men, particularly the Americans, were really suffering as a result. I had made friends with a number of the chaps from the USA and found that they were fascinated and amused by my impersonation of an old type English butler. On a few occasions I was told in all seriousness that I would easily obtain employment in the States in this capacity. Names and addresses were readily written out and given to me, but alas, somewhere along the way I lost them.

A young Mexican, who had enlisted in order to gain American nationality, gave me a ring as a keepsake, engraved with the word Juarez. I still have the ring and remember the man's name; it was Porfie Yvarra.

There was an occasion when I was visiting an English lad in one of the brick dormitories and felt, rather than saw, someone's eyes on me. On turning around I perceived that I was the object of interest to an American chap about the same height and weight as myself. That fact was not as apparent then as it was later. He smiled and said, 'sorry to be caught staring at you, but I'd just love to take your jacket home as a souvenir!' He was referring of course, to my battledress blouse with its entire airborne insignia sewn on it. He went on: 'I've noticed you a few times in the camp and wondered if you'd mind swapping with me?' The battledress blouse was an extremely practical item of clothing, but unlined, and it did very little to keep out the intense cold. Our camouflage smocks had been taken from us because the Germans said they were regarded as escape equipment. The item of clothing which was offered in exchange for my blouse was a waterproof khaki-lined zipped jacket. I thought the proposition over for all of two minutes and then started to remove my blouse. The Yank was so delighted that he threw in a couple of medal ribbons as well. I wore them throughout my term as a PoW.

Without claiming to have started a trend, from that moment I noticed a great deal of equipment changing hands, especially jackets and boots. The style of American boot most in favour with our lads was the paratrooper boot. We had no special footwear issued as Paras, having had to make do with the good old sturdy British 'ammunition boot' as it was called. The Americans wore lace-up boots that covered the calf as well. They looked very smart but I remembered having heard a word of warning from an English lad who had already made the exchange. 'They might look alright,' he had said, 'but my feet are bloody cold!' This was the problem; apparently the American boot did not keep the feet nearly as warm in that awful winter as the well-made British Army issue. The fact was borne out several times when rueful Britons regretted that they had rashly made the swap.

It was on a dry, sunny but cold day that I made my application to join an outside working party. Apart from longing for a change of scene to relieve the boredom, I also felt the need to exercise my body. Like most other men, I hated being locked up and knew that if the opportunity presented itself I would make the most of it and attempt to escape. With the war so obviously near its end, and there being no doubt as to who the victors would be, it may seem strange, even stupid, to someone who has not been incarcerated, for me to consider 'going over the wall'. The feeling I had was almost like a sickness and was getting worse every day. Optimist that I was, I still did not consider that the chance would present itself first time out, but I just had to get outside that bloody awful camp, if only for a few hours.

A sergeant major of my acquaintance was responsible for compiling the lists of out-workers, subject to German approval. So after a word with him I found myself being marched out of camp with fourteen or fifteen others. We marched through the town, which was badly damaged, until we came to the railway station. This really was in a mess, having been bombed quite recently.

Our job was to clear the rubble from the approach road so as to make it possible for vehicles to drive up and to leave the station. Tools were supplied in the shape of long-handled shovels and wheelbarrows. Nobody was trying to break any production records and the guard seemed content to let us work at our own pace. As long as we kept moving there was no complaint.

The sound of a train pulling in to the station caught our attention and between shovels-full we were watching the passengers emerge from the large station entrance, which was still standing. Shouts of hilarity prompted us to watch more closely to see a number of Hitler Youth members running and jumping out onto the road. Their shouts died when they saw us and they sauntered in our direction, we thought, to satisfy their curiosity. Discretion dictated that we ignore them so we turned again to our labours. The Hitler Youth lads were standing immediately behind us as we were shovelling away, when one bolder than the rest, or less discreet, gave one of our workmates a full-blooded kick in the backside. It was a very painful kick, made more so by virtue of it being unexpected. The offender stood his ground, laughing hilariously.

Straightening up, and then putting down his shovel rather slowly, the Para swung round and in the same movement punched the youth right in the mouth! Looks of sheer disbelief registered on the faces of his comrades, as he swung away spitting blood and teeth. Expecting some sort of retaliation we bunched together gripping our tools. All the Hitler Youth wore side arms, even though they looked to be only fifteen or sixteen years old. Our group would have stood little chance if their guns had been fired. At this point however, our guard intervened, by stepping between the two factions making it very plain that they had him to reckon with if they were hoping to exact revenge. It was clear that the guard felt that justice had been done and that the matter should go no further. That was the only time that I went out on a working party at Limburg.

Chapter Fourteen

Stalag IVB Mühlberg

T wo days later I was told to prepare myself for another move. It was during these two days that word seeped through somehow that other ranks – that is non-commissioned officers and men – could now wear ties with their uniforms. This had been a privilege previously granted only to officers. How the information came through to us I never knew, but it turned out to be correct.

It seems rather ridiculous now in retrospect, that so many of us became practically obsessed with the desire to implement this latest War Office instruction. Pieces of material were in very short supply in PoW camp but one enterprising lad came up with the answer. American Army shirts had been supplied by the Red Cross for issue to all ranks including British Troops. Some of them were the thick khaki winter shirts while others were a lighter material in colour and texture, for use in summer. These had collars too. The inventive lad had realized that there was an overlapping piece of material which ran down inside the front of all these shirts, the idea being to fasten this before buttoning up the front of the shirt.[1] This strip removed from the shirt, provided more than enough material to make a useable tie. It was a simple matter to cut it out with care, and the chaps with light shirts swapped their pieces with the men who had the darker khaki ones. Being handy with a needle I was kept quite busy up to

1. This piece of additional shirt material acted as a 'gas flap' and was designed to add an additional layer of protection against mustard gas.

the moment of my departure from Limburg. It sounds like a trivial subject to discuss at such length, but the reader must understand that time hung very heavily on unoccupied minds and hands. Time was the enemy in PoW camps, not necessarily the Germans.

Whether we were transported from Limburg by train or truck I cannot remember and must apologize for the mental block which prevents me recalling this aspect of my captivity. It seems even stranger to me knowing that I can recall almost everything else that occurred whilst a prisoner. I could, of course, have lied about it, but feel compelled to write about my experiences truthfully as they come to me.

There were a hundred or so forming the group that departed from that really dreadful camp. Our destination, we learned, was Stalag IVB Mühlberg[2]. The weather was kinder on our arrival, though still very, very cold, but it did not rain as it had at the previous place. Delays occurred though and we were told that this was due to our having to be re-registered – groans at this – and that we were to be passed through a de-lousing unit – cheer at that! There was not a man among us, no matter how careful or fastidious he had been about his personal cleanliness, who was not swarming with lice. At last we went through the formalities of registering, and that completed, passed on into a large building adjoining the office block. Every item of clothing was removed and hung on a large coat-hanger. This in turn was hung, with others, on a huge wheeled rack. This was pushed into a massive oven. The doors were closed and the heat turned on.

Stark naked as we were we felt very vulnerable and were getting colder by the minute until, after a few minutes, we formed a queue

---

2. Stammlager IVB was situated 80km north-west of Dresden and was the home of over 300,000 prisoners of war from over 40 nations between 1941 and 1945.

and filed into the shower room. Hot water was turned on by remote control; it was sheer luxury; bliss; heaven.

There was no apparent hurry; we were the last batch to go through, so we were allowed to have a long hot soak. Marvellous! Emerging from the showers at the opposite end of the oven we collected our clothes and after drying off and dressing we entered into the camp proper. It was huge. A dirt road ran through our section of the Stalag and we marched along this road, stopping every now and then whilst the German NCO allocated us in ones and twos to one or other of the large huts on either side. An Allied NCO had been put in charge of each hut and it was from these men that we learned where we would sleep. Bunk beds, three high, or maybe four, were lined along both sides of the hut with two large stoves in the middle, and a wash house dividing it from a similar building at the far end.

Bed boards supported a very thin mattress of straw, but the boards were in short supply owing to the fact that cooking required fuel and boards had been pinched to do that cooking. Always a gregarious person I soon befriended another chap from my home town of Liverpool. Bill lived two tram stops from the house my parents had moved into just after the war had begun. He was from a Para battalion and with two other Paras, both Welshmen, we decided to pool our resources and generally look out for each other.

Early on I had realized that my bed was full of lice so I decided not to sleep on it and chose the nearby hard table instead. It may not have been as comfortable at night as the bed but it was certainly more comfortable during the day. One could see, with some wry amusement, numbers of men in the large compound during daylight hours, all scratching themselves. Having been rid of the horrid things on entry into camp I had no wish to resume acquaintance with them.

Every Allied nationality was represented at Mühlberg but the people I remember most clearly are the Russians. Now and again we would be issued with Red Cross parcels to do with as we wished. These supplemented the meagre rations of soup and bread we were given every day. No parcels for the Russians though, and it's doubtful that they were ever given the same rations as we were getting. A great number of them had lost legs, arms or feet. There seemed to be a lot of them with no feet, probably due to frost-bite. A picture forever etched on my memory is of a Russian without feet, getting along on his knees, trying to jump up to steal potatoes from a high-sided wagon as it drove through the camp. Some of our lads would wait in ambush – so to speak – sneak up to the wagon, pinch some spuds and then give them to the starving Russians, this in spite of their own acute hunger.

All Airborne men were ordered to parade at a point near the main entrance one day. Some of us thought the worst, but were assured that if any attempt was made to march us out of the camp, then the whole place would rise up in protest. Such extreme measures were not necessary however, for what took place next! A huge staff car was parked outside the gate and when we had all assembled the gate was opened and the car, bearing a high-ranking officer, drove into the compound.

The officer tapped the driver on the shoulder; the driver brought the car to a halt within three sides of the square we now formed. He stood up and I recognized him immediately. It was Field Marshal Model who had harangued me in another age it seemed, but months ago in Holland.

Through an interpreter he told us what a good fight we had fought and not to be ashamed of having been taken prisoner. Look forward to the end of the war with pride; we could go home with our heads high. There was more in a similar vein; he spoke for about ten minutes. As he drove away, I could not help thinking that it must be rare, in the annals of war, for an enemy General to congratulate the defeated enemy on their proficiency at arms. It was with not a little sadness that I heard he had committed suicide some time later; he was, I believe wanted by the Russians for war crimes.

Mühlberg was blessed with a very efficient escape committee, which seemed to concentrate on getting out members of RAF aircrew. This may have been due to instructions received from the War Office, but that is pure speculation. A favourite ploy was to approach a man who was to go out to another smaller camp as part of a labour force. He was then asked if he would change places with an RAF man. If they agreed they would swap identities. Someone would break into the admin buildings and change over the photographs of the men concerned onto the other documents. In the morning as the party departed, they would be checked in single file through the gate and a quick scrutiny at the photograph would determine that the right man was leaving. By this time, of course, the RAF man would be dressed as a soldier. Some members of aircrew had been prisoners for a long time and quite often a soldier impersonating say, an air gunner, would find himself receiving parcels addressed to the would-be escaper.

Idling time away in the hut one evening, I was addressed by a senior NCO. The hut was not very well lit but I could see that he had an air force chap with him. The NCO asked me if I had put my name down to go out to a labour camp.

Not wishing to sound rude, I curbed my impulse to ask what business it was of his. Rank meant very little in a Stalag anyway. I answered that I had not yet put my name down but intended to do so in the near future. 'When you do, would you consider swapping?' he said, and without more ado he asked the other man to come forward into the better light. The likeness was incredible; it was like looking into a mirror but seeing myself in RAF uniform. 'As you can see we wouldn't have to change the photographs,' the NCO explained. I confess that I was taken aback, but recovering said that I too wanted to escape. Nothing more was said. They both shook my hand and left the hut.

Food in such a place was at a premium and all of one's belongings were precious because one way or another they could be converted by trading for something to eat. Therefore stealing was treated very seriously and punished very harshly. The thief would be made to stand in a corner of the wash house and anyone inclined would hit him with fists or anything else handy. It was not surprising when a man died under this treatment, because there was no shortage of men to carry out the punishment.

Items of clothing most needed by the Germans were boots, especially British Army boots, whose reputation was well established. The German boot being made from some strange ersatz material did not keep out the cold of that bitter winter. It was vital, therefore, that in order to prevent their boots being stolen, men simply had to sleep with them. This remedy also had the advantage, on a cold morning, of having warm boots to put one's feet into when rising. Sometimes in the night there would be a scuffle when a man, driven desperate by hunger, would try to steal another's boots or some other item of kit, which could be traded for food or some other essential.

Christmas of 1944 arrived while I was in Mühlberg and not wanting the occasion to go by without some celebration, we decided to make a plum pudding. Pooling our ration of black bread was not a hardship. The job of cooking was given to me, no cordon bleu chef. I crumbled the bread into small pieces, mixed it with sugar and prunes from the Red Cross, managed to make a steaming pan from odds and ends, then cooked it for forty-eight hours. Yes, forty-eight! One of us kept an all night vigil the first night and I performed the same duty the second night. Scrounging for fuel was left to the other members of the group while the fourth kept watch. Water had to be brought from the wash house to ensure that it didn't boil dry. This was rather difficult at night when only one man was on duty. It was quite impossible to keep an eye on the stove the entire time, when collecting water. All went well and we ate the pudding on Christmas Day as planned. It was delicious even allowing for our jaded palates.

Rumour was always rife in such surroundings. Sometimes it was proved true but mostly it was the product of someone's vivid imagination. So when we heard that Polish women were arriving, we put it down to the latter cause. In this instance we were wrong. A Russian compound was cleared of its occupants, they being crammed into an already over-crowded compound elsewhere, and then through the gates came a streaming mass of young women. In those circumstances every woman would look attractive, but some of them were real beauties. They were hustled quickly into their compound and there we were with a wire fence between us trying to communicate. Food was thrown over to them and judging by the way it was fought over and then eaten, they had not been fed for a long time. Someone told me later that a Polish pilot in our camp strolled over to see what the excitement was all about and found himself looking at his wife through the wire. His reaction can only be imagined, particularly when he heard the rumour that these girls had been forcibly recruited to staff German military brothels.

Bill and I made a point every day, weather permitting, of walking round the compound two or three times for exercise. We returned to the hut earlier than anticipated one day because it looked as if it might rain. Our Welsh companions were standing close to the shelf on which our foodstuffs were stored and looking very guilty. Being sharp Liverpudlians, Bill and I immediately realized what was happening. Going up to them I asked them a question which need a prompt reply. It was obvious that they could not answer because they each had something in their mouths. They had been caught stealing our food!

Terrified of the possible consequences, previously mentioned, they began to grovel. It needed only a word from Bill or me and they would have been marched into the wash house and they knew it.

In all conscience, I could not be responsible for the beating up and possible death of another man in those circumstances. We Liverpool lads stepped outside, talked it over and returned to the Welsh chaps with a proposition. A proposition I might add, that they couldn't really refuse. Their indiscretion was to go unreported but ALL the food stayed with us. They accepted with bad grace but knew that the alternative was far worse. Shortly after this, with our association ended, they were granted a transfer to another hut.

Entertainments in Mühlberg were provided by the numerous talented men of so many races. Comedians, jugglers, musicians, singers and even a hypnotist. They came along to the huts and put their talents on display and the level of professionalism was very high.

There was an Irish chap who had a beautiful tenor voice but whose repertoire was limited. Every time he was asked to sing, it was the same song with no variation. 'This is a lovely way to spend an evening'. It was hardly appropriate in those surroundings. The camp hypnotist paid us a visit and asked for volunteers to submit to his will, emphasizing that it would help him considerably if the subject did not 'fight him'. Not wanting to be made to look foolish as they suspected they would, the lads stayed in their seats. More out of sympathy for the hypnotist I stepped forward followed by two or three more. Sitting me down in front of him, he asked me not to oppose his will and added that he would do nothing to embarrass me. Having said that he then went on to tell me what he proposed to do. 'I'm going to put you to sleep; when I snap my fingers you will open your eyes, take that mug off the shelf, go into the wash house and fill it with water. Then you will bring it back here and put it down in its original place.'

It happened just as he had said, but I am not going to suggest that I followed his simple instructions in an unknowing trance. I was totally aware of everything that I was doing; the strange thing to me was that when I attempted to diverge from the hypnotist's directions I found that I couldn't! Initially I tried to pick up the wrong mug, but my hand never completed its journey. It only went towards the specific one nominated. Then when I was half-way between the wash house door and the tap, I stopped with the intention of turning round. My feet felt as though they were glued to the floor! Only when I went once more towards the tap would they move. Again when the mug was half-full I tried to pull it away from under the tap. Nothing doing there either! I emphasize that I was fully aware of what I was doing but could not move the mug until it was full as he had instructed. On my return, having replaced the mug, I sat down again and was made to perform a card trick while still under the influence.

A card was put into my hand and I was told to 'weigh it' and put it back into the pack which was shuffled by a member of the audience. One at a time the cards were laid onto my hand until I identified the original chosen card. It was a most impressive performance from the hypnotist. He had other volunteers doing similar simple things and when I spoke to a couple of them afterwards, they both agreed that they knew what they were doing but lacked the will to change any of the instructions.

During these evening entertainments men in one hut would invite mates from another to visit and would spend a little time together when the show was over. A man from the hut directly opposite to ours was spending some time with a pal from his unit and only when he felt that it was time to go home did he realize that it was well past curfew.

The simple solution was for him to stay overnight with us; a bed was found for him and the men settled down until the morning. Bright and early the lad rose in order to get some breakfast before the first roll call of the day. Stepping out of our hut, he did not see the guard who was standing in the lee of the building. He was halfway across the road when the sentry ordered him to halt. Surprised, he turned to face the German and was bayoneted to death where he stood. There were witnesses to this brutal act. Some of the chaps from our hut had heard the sentry call out and went to the door to see what was going on.

There was hell to pay. The guard, aware that he had grossly overstepped the mark and sensing the mood of the men, stopped when he reached the pedestrian gate. The guard there quickly opened up and he darted through. The gate was rapidly re-locked.

Without doubt I can say that had we got our hands on that man, he would have been strung up. Representations were made to the commandant, but as in a previous less serious case, we never saw the murderer again. Informed that he had been posted to the Russian Front, two or three days later, we could do nothing more than report it to the Red Cross Committee when they next visited.

The cold weather persisted and seemed to get worse, possibly due to our reserves dwindling which meant that our bodies could not fight back against the elements. Roll-calls seemed to be longer, which the Germans didn't mind; apparently it passed their day for them. We didn't take too kindly to standing about in the conditions, and mumbles of discontent became louder as we got colder and colder. All this helped to make up my mind to apply for inclusion on a working party. There was a long waiting list, I was told, but I still insisted on my name being put on it.

Radios in camp – quite illegal – informed us that the enemy was making a push on the Ardennes and was having some success against the American troops opposing them. Within days the Germans ordered us to clear out some of the huts, as a great number of American prisoners were to arrive soon. They arrived that night outside the main gates, but did not come into the camp areas because the commandant thought it too late to put them through the registering procedure and the de-lousing centre. The simple solution was to herd them all into the woods not far from the camp, throw an armed cordon around it and hold these poor lads there until morning. So bitter was the cold that it killed them off like flies. Apparently most of them made no attempt to fight it; they just lay down and succumbed.

For days thereafter, working parties were going out to bury them and as my name was on the working party list now, I was called upon to perform this heart-breaking task also.

My friend Bill had, by this time, traded places with a potential escaper, and was dressed in RAF uniform. He had also started receiving parcels in the name of his assumed identity and was sharing them with me. On the face of it, a fairly cushy number, but something was eating at me; my feet were getting itchy again and would not be denied. I started pushing again to be included in a working party very soon, and my persistence was rewarded. There was just time for Bill and I to exchange addresses, grab my few articles of kit, and run for one of the lorries that were to take exactly one hundred of us away from Mühlberg. I do remember starting that journey in a lorry but am not sure if we went all the way in it. As far as I know we did, the trip ending at a small town in Saxony – Borna.

Chapter Fifteen

Borna

There was a huge open-cast coalmine on the outskirts of the town of Borna[1] and our camp was in the shadow of one of the factories which manufactured briquettes from the coal wrested from the massive hole in the ground. A new hut had been built for us, divided into four sections; each section housed twenty five men. All told there were seven hundred PoWs at this camp: four hundred French, one hundred Russians and, including us, two hundred British. The nationalities were separated by high wire fences but there was considerable traffic between us and the French. None at all, officially, involved the Russians. The other hundred Brits were 'old' prisoners, in the sense that they had been captured much earlier in the war. They lived in the other hut in our compound. Pleased to see us, they made us welcome and, having been informed of our impending arrival, had prepared meals for us. A great sacrifice we thought. Two Liverpool lads were my hosts and they were most kind. Undoubtedly some of the food was from Red Cross parcels but other ingredients were locally grown. However this attitude of friendship changed very quickly!

After the initial welcome, when these lads realized that our presence meant closer captivity for them, we became the butt of their deep displeasure and an atmosphere developed between the two factions which was most unpleasant, even to the point of loudly

---

1. Borna is near Leipzig in the state of Saxony.

condemning the opening of the second front. It was explained to us that before our invasion of Europe, all these lads had good jobs in the town, were well fed, and in most cases had girlfriends! They now deeply resented having to spend most of their days under the eye of an armed guard, when before they had been allowed to come and go as they pleased. From then on there was a tacit agreement to have nothing to do with each other!

The hut was equipped with twelve double bunks and a single bed on which the hut marshal slept. A large coal-burning stove stood in a central position and there was a door which, when opened, revealed a large coal bunker. The German attitude was, surprisingly, that as we were helping to produce the coal we could have as much as we needed to keep warm and cook. In this respect we were better off than the civilian population in the nearby town. While I was there we were never short of fuel for the greedy stove. Working clothes were issued too so that we could now wash our uniforms and keep them smart and tidy. The American jacket I had acquired stood me in good stead during the terribly cold days. At no time did I regret making the swap.

Most of our guards were *Volkssturm* men, the German equivalent of our Home Guard: men too old and boys too young or disabled to be able to fight in a front line unit. There was a sprinkling of tougher young men, but for the most part they were men who had fought in the previous war of 1914-18. The officer in charge of the camp was there only for a short time after our arrival. He was posted to the dreaded Russian Front and a lowly corporal took over. A rather sickly looking German soldier was the official interpreter whose English was rather fractured and who persisted in calling everyone 'my darlings' in English.

They all seemed to be impressed by the two medal ribbons on my jacket beneath which I had now added a pair of Para wings and an Airborne Divisional sign, the Winged Pegasus. They were never enlightened to the fact that I was not entitled to the ribbons.

At Borna I formed a friendship with a chap from one of the parachute battalions. His surname was Gregory – shortened to Greg, I never knew his first name. He had an addiction which could have proved fatal then and I am sure has done so by now! Greg would literally rather smoke than eat, even to the point of swapping his meagre rations for tobacco. To their credit, the British soon cottoned on and even the non-smokers with Red Cross cigarettes to spare refused to trade with him. Not so the French! Food was food from whatever source, and so every evening after work I would accompany Greg into the French compound. There were two reasons for my doing this, the first was to urge him every step of the way to eat the food – a futile exercise this. The other reason was to see that he was not short changed. The French had no scruples in that respect either.

I worked in a team of twelve men. We were marched out of the camp every morning with one armed guard, turned left outside the gate towards the town, and having passed a few of the houses on the outskirts, turned right taking a route towards the railway goods sidings. This eventually took us to the far side of the open cast mine and our place of work. On the top level as we were, our job was to keep the excavator going along its tracks by lifting the rails from behind it and then re-laying them in front of the machine. However, the ground was frozen so solid that we also had to light huge fires, using briquettes for fuel, so that the ground would thaw enough for the excavator to tackle it.

It was while we were standing around one of these fires to get warm again that Herr Schmidt, the civilian ganger, ordered us back to work. This specimen had been a PoW in England during the First World War and, for reasons unexplained, the experience had soured him. He took a very dim view of Englishmen and an even dimmer view of Englishmen who would not toil for the Fatherland. The other lads drifted reluctantly away from the fire but I gave Schmidt the Churchill 'V' sign and held my ground. He was furious. How dare anyone mock his authority! As quick as Wyatt Earp he drew a gun from his pocket and pointed it at me. 'Steffans,' he said loudly, 'get back to work or I'll shoot!' I bent down to pick up my shovel not to work but to hit him with. One of the lads sensed this and rushing forward, pulled me away from the fire. 'Steffans' was the nearest Schmidt could ever get to pronouncing my surname. The silly thing I remember about this incident is the piece of cloth hanging from the muzzle of the pistol, put there to keep it clean.

Down below us, in the mine proper, was a really huge excavator. I was told by a proud German that it was the biggest in the world and I believed him. The machine ran on three sets of tracks while another two sets supported the trains of open trucks being filled with coal. However, until the top layer of soil had been removed by hand, the main excavator could not operate. Its sole purpose was to dig coal but without us it was useless.

There were frequent breakdowns. Not all of them, by any means, accidental. Schmidt would be dancing about with anger, knowing that we were responsible but having no way to prove it.

Red Cross parcels were being issued at the rate of one for two men every fortnight and the Germans would tell us that our bombers were to blame. It is true that at that stage of the war we had total air superiority and we knew that railways were among the prime targets the bombers went for. We were not, however, quite convinced and the work, the hard work that we were asked to do was wearing us down. Greg, with his preference for smoking rather than eating, was wasting away before my eyes. It was impossible to ignore his condition and I gave him what food I could spare, which was very little. Survival was the name of the game now and number one came first. The time arrived when he was so obviously unfit for work that something had to be done. It was he who came up with the desperate solution. 'If you wallop me on the ankle with a pickaxe,' he said, 'I won't be able to walk, never mind work!' I thought he was mad, and told him so, but he convinced me that he meant it and I reluctantly agreed to help him.

Drawing the line at hitting him with something as hefty as a pickaxe, I suggested that an iron bar be used so that I could hit him exactly how and where he wanted me to. Although I realized that by doing as he asked I was helping him, because he was in such a dreadful physical condition, it was not an easy decision for me to make. While agreeing with Greg, I intended putting off the whole nasty business for as long as possible. He would not be denied though and insisted on my doing the deed the following morning as soon as we arrived at our work area. This was the time when Schmidt had a chat with the guard who had marched us to the site. It certainly seemed to be the ideal opportunity but it was only the depth of Greg's desperation that convinced me that it had to be done.

Picking up the iron bar that we had hidden a few days earlier, and knowing that a gentle tap was not what he wanted, I brought it round and down on Greg's right ankle. His cry of anguish was quite genuine, I had really walloped him. Throwing away the bar and reaching for my pickaxe I stood beside him looking contrite. Startled by the loud cries, Schmidt came bustling across to us, saw what appeared to have happened and ran back to the guard for a hurried consultation. The guard actually ran to the nearest phone and summoned a vehicle from the camp. It was a flat-bed lorry but Greg did not complain. Though still in great pain he managed a wink in my direction as he was helped aboard.

The doctor was summoned from Borna to look at Greg's injury, gave him a week in the camp hospital and returned him to work when seven days were up. There was no possibility of our repeating the performance. Even Schmidt, thick as he was, would not have been fooled by the same thing happening again to the same man. It was while Greg was nearing the end of his week in hospital that I too wanted a day off. The camp hospital did have a permanent medical orderly and although German he seemed to be quite sympathetic when we reported sick with minor ailments. My sneezing fit led to a severe cold which I was afraid might develop into 'flu' again, so I went to see this chap in the Medical Inspection Room. He wrote me out a note for the German corporal excusing me from labour for that day, with the injunction to see him again the following day if I felt no better. Although the weather hadn't lost its bite, it was a bright sunny day, which was shattered by the sound of the local air raid sirens. It was the first time we had heard them since arriving at Borna and, in fact, we had been told by the Germans that Borna had never been bombed during the course of the war.

Walking to the door of the hut I looked up into the clear blue sky and saw a solitary American Flying Fortress. Its route lay right over the town and even as I watched I saw its bombs fall. There was a slight upward movement of the plane in its flight, having been relieved of its bomb-load, but otherwise it maintained its course. Not a gun was fired at it, probably because the Germans felt there was no need to defend the town, as it had not been attacked before. Before I could observe more or arrive at any other conclusion a sentry ran over to me from the gate and insisted on me accompanying him to the air raid shelter. 'A little late!' I thought wryly, as there was only one plane. I picked up Greg on the way past the camp hospital and with the guard hurrying ahead, we entered the shaft that housed the huge conveyor belt for bringing the coal into the factory. This was our air raid shelter. We were to get to know it better very soon.

There is a lasting impression that every German guard at Borna, without exception, felt that during an air raid the planes had singled him out personally for destruction. On every occasion thereafter, when we were ordered to the shelter, the guards ran ahead of us. So much for the brave master race!

Although we had heard that the Nazis had done their best, or worst, to abolish religion we were always allowed to rest on Sundays, so it was the day we all looked forward to. It was on a Sunday, two days after the air raid, that Greg was discharged from hospital. I helped him with his pitifully few belongings and we tried to think of some way we could reduce his work load. We both knew that if he was declared totally unfit for work then he would be posted back to a larger camp, possibly Mühlberg. He accepted that rather than have that happen he would just have to bluff his way along out on the site.

On Monday we resumed work at about 6.30am and were going about our duties in our usual lethargic way when we saw a guard from the camp hurrying towards us. He carried out a muttered conversation with Schmidt and then stood off to one side, obviously waiting. The ganger called us all to him with a shout, and without preamble selected six of us to go with the guard, instructing us to take picks and shovels. In our limited German we tried to extract information from the guard, but he just shook his head as he led us towards to the town. Puzzled, we walked through the neat streets under the curious gaze of the populace and it was with very mixed feelings that we followed the guard into the town cemetery.

Here we were greeted coldly by a uniformed officer of the TODT Organization, the German labour force. An area had been marked out with white tape and this fat officious oaf ordered us to start digging. After a few minutes one of our lads started snivelling. 'What's up with you?' I asked. 'We're digging our own grave!' he said, 'This is retaliation for the bombing the other day.' All of my efforts to shut him up were in vain. He was quite convinced that we were to be killed and buried in the hole we were now excavating and it seemed he was beginning to convince some of the others. I too began to have my doubts and told them that in the event of our being told to line up in front of an armed party of Germans we were not to simply and meekly submit. We had shovels and picks and I was determined to use them.

It quickly became apparent however, that the hole we were digging was far too big for six people. There was a short break for lunch, much resented by the brown uniformed TODT officer, but the surprise here was that the lowly guard seemed to have the authority to override him. Another surprise was when German women came into the cemetery bringing food for us and then staying a while to chat.

Lunch over, we resumed our digging and were almost down to the required depth when a lorry drove into the cemetery carrying, among other things, three long poles. We were allowed to carry on with our labours while the lorry was unloaded by the three men who had ridden on it. There were sounds of more digging close by, and then we saw that they were flag poles. A tall one in the centre and a smaller one on either side. Ropes had been attached before the poles had been erected and soon a Nazi flag, bearing the hated Swastika, was flying from all three. A podium too came off the lorry and was placed in position.

From our position in the communal grave, we eyed all these preparations covertly, wondering what the hell was going on. Another larger lorry drove into the cemetery, its load covered by tarpaulin. It met the smaller lorry which was on the way out and there was a lot of unseemly shouting, backing and revving up before the new lorry could drive to a position near the grave. Ropes were untied and the tarpaulin thrown to one side to reveal a number of coffins packed tightly together. It was then that we knew that these were civilian victims of the haphazard bombing of a few days earlier and for whom the large grave was intended. Right up to that moment, though, there had been doubts, even in my mind.

The TODT officer walked round to the rim of the hole in which we six stood, possibly to assess if it came up to his requirements, then, apparently satisfied he gestured to us to join him at ground level. This man conducted the whole proceedings completely without emotion; at no time did he betray that he was moved in any way by the fact that he was burying a number of his fellow Germans.

Walking over to the lorry, and after a brief conversation with the driver, he then indicated that we were to unload the coffins. There was something unethical about this aspect of the business to me. Here we were six scruffy prisoners of war, the enemy in fact, being asked to handle coffins containing the remains of people killed by our allies. Even had we been averse to doing the job there was no way out of it. Two men climbed up on to the wagon bed and started clumsily shifting the coffins to a position where we four could ease them off the lorry. It was obvious by the weight that a whole body was not in some of the caskets. Most of them were lightweight plywood, state supplied, with ill-fitting lids but two others were heavy, elaborate affairs which needed all six of us to move over to the grave.

Any time now, I thought, we'll be dismissed, feeling that our presence might prove embarrassing. I was wrong. We were destined to stay throughout the whole business, even to placing the coffins in the grave. This exposed a problem – there was not enough space for all the caskets.

The size of the two larger ones had thrown out the calculations of the brown-shirted officer. Only he could make the decision as to what should be done, and he resolved the problem by ordering two of the cheaper ones to be put on top of the others. A crowd had gathered by this time, the time of the burial obviously having been publicized. There was absolutely no resentment shown at our presence by any number of the sizeable gathering. In fact a well-dressed lady started to talk to me, but from what I understood of her conversation, she was feeling sorrier for herself than the victims or their relatives. Disgusted by her selfish attitude I stressed that my home town was Liverpool. She turned on her heels and walked away.

The TODT officer mounted the podium and began to address the crowd; he made little impression on them, the whole political harangue falling on deaf ears. They were there to pay their respects to the dead, not to hear that their friends and relatives had died in support of a lost cause. Realizing that he was wasting his time, the officer cut short his speech, gathered up his papers, and waving a hand to indicate that he wanted us to fill in the grave, he stalked off.

Some of the people remained until we had finished the final act of the solemn proceedings, but most had made their way out of the cemetery by the time we had finished. The incongruity of our situation was not lost on me, particularly when some of the bereaved thanked us for what we had done. Too late to return to the work site, we suggested to the guard that we take our tools to the camp and then carry them to the job in the morning. He accepted this and through the gathering dusk we walked to the Stalag, rather subdued by all that we had heard that day.

Hunger remained our greatest enemy. However every night a large bad-tempered Alsatian dog was turned loose in the compound to ensure there was no traffic between the Russians and us. They were not allowed outside their hut at all when darkness had fallen, but as our toilets were a few yards away from the hut in which we slept, we were compelled by calls of nature to venture out into the night. Two of our chaps had seen the dog as a source of food and with this in mind had started feeding it tit-bits on their way to the lavatory. An empty stomach can quiet a vociferous conscience so with a pair of stolen wire cutters they opened up the dividing wire one very dark night, coaxed the dog into our compound and hit it on the head with a pick handle.

Even a large dog does not go far among one hundred hungry men. It just disappeared! The inedible parts just dumped into the deep pit of the lavatory. The Germans, of course found the cut wire and therefore knew roughly which direction the dog had taken, but even they, I feel, did not or could not, bring themselves to accept that the animal-loving British would kill and eat a dog!

Potatoes being unloaded from a goods wagon at the railway sidings were being spilled on to the ground as we walked past on our way to work. The guard started to unship his rifle and bayonet from his shoulder, ready for trouble. Ignoring him I dived for the spuds and started thrusting them into the front of my jacket. The other lads plunged to gather up the unexpected bounty too and the guard, acknowledging the futility of any action he might take, stood back looking anxiously to the left and right. To add to my luck that day, on the way back to camp in the evening I found a small rabbit, frozen solid in nature's deep freeze. That night I ate well, having skinned, gutted and cooked it myself.

Romance could blossom, even in that male-dominated environment. A lovely petite Polish girl was working as a slave labourer on a nearby farm and occasionally drove by our work site with an aged horse in the shafts of a decrepit cart. Though I had begun to pick up some German words, my vocabulary was still very limited. Sometimes words are not necessary though. Why she should pick me to be her lover remains a mystery to this day. There were men on the work party, taller and more handsome than me and she could have chosen any one of them.

Yes! Sex – physical love-making did occur, but most of the time it was meaningful glances, hand holding and rash promises which anyone would have made in those circumstances. I often wonder what happened to her, but today I cannot even remember her name.

The relentless grip of winter was easing its hold on the land. This made our job easier, but more significantly we knew it was bringing the Allied armies nearer. It was clear that the local Germans were terrified that the Russians would reach the area before the Americans.

There were no secret radios at Borna as far as I knew but by this time the guards were becoming more talkative, and much that they told us turned out to be true. There were air raids every night now and when someone asked me if I knew what type of planes were coming over, it gave me an idea; I couldn't tell them but thought of a way that I could find out!

The hut had a two door set up so as to maintain the night time black-out. On entering the hut the first door opened inwards in the usual way. There was a six foot long space and then a second door on the left which opened directly into the hut. This space had a ceiling to it and access to the space above this ceiling could be gained via the coal house door inside. It was a simple matter to stand up on the heap of briquettes and jump up into the space. So I had the notion that next time the sirens started braying their litany, and during the confusion of everyone running for the shelter, I would hide in this place until all was quiet again, then I would emerge. That night, sure enough, the sirens started up when we were in bed, the guards came dashing in shouting 'Raus, Raus!' They then dashed off to the other billets to chase the other occupants up as well. The poor old Russkies were left to fend for themselves, by the way, locked up in their hut during the entire air raid.

All the lights went out, the master switch having been thrown in the corporal's office. The inside of the building was quite dark now, but outside the gloom was relieved by the sweeping searchlights. I made a play of supervising the exodus but as soon as the last man was through the door I bolted back in and scrambled up to my hiding place. When all sounds of human proximity had faded, I hopped down and went to the window to watch for the searchlights picking out potential targets. On the first night, I saw quite clearly the ghostly shapes of four-engine bombers, Lancasters. But as the weeks passed they were two-engine fighter bombers. The greatest thrill came when I was looking up into the night sky where I distinctly saw the shapes of three Spitfires.

That meant the Allies were really very close. I was so excited on this occasion that I was about to run outside, thinking everyone, guards included, would be in the shelter. I was wrong, opening the door inside the hut revealed the outer door standing open. Framed in the doorway was the largest German guard on the camp, with his back to me. He was built like the proverbial brick outhouse. The noise from the planes and guns covered any sound I had made so I remained undetected but I had no idea how he would react if he found me there. Discretion being the better part etc, I stepped back into the billet, closing the door unnecessarily quietly. It was impossible for him to have heard me. Not wanting to risk climbing into my hiding place again, I crawled under one of the beds. Unlikely though it seems I dozed off and was wakened in the grey light of dawn when the other chaps returned from the shelter. They were delighted when I told them I had seen the Spitfires and there were cries of 'it won't be long now!'

It was Greg who broached the subject first – ESCAPE! My desire to get away had been somewhat subdued by the fact that I was leaving camp every day except Sunday. Once my friend had raised the subject, however, I started to think more about it. Looking back, with all the benefit of hindsight, it was stupid at that stage of the war to even contemplate it. The Allies were so obviously winning the war, all we had to do was sit tight and let them come to us. Put it down to my itchy feet or a sense of adventure that I had not acknowledged. I just do not know what made me abandon a safe billet and take off into the unknown.

Having established that the Russians had reached the far side of the river Elbe it seemed logical to head that way. It really must have been among the most badly planned escape attempts of the war; even after the passage of so many years, my hackles rise when

I think about it. Thrusting what food we had into a kit bag I now owned, we simply crossed the compound towards the toilet block and, going behind it, opened up the wire and crawled through. That was it! Nothing dramatic like digging a tunnel, going out in disguise, or even having prepared documents. God does often take care of fools, there's no doubt about it. He took care of us alright. With only a general idea in which direction the river lay, we started our hazardous journey. The night gave us cover so we kept going through the darkness, crossing fields, roads and streams.

Dawn found us in a copse, so we had a debate as to what we should do next. A major factor in our considerations was Greg's physical condition and I felt that this alone should have been enough to put a stop to this nonsense before it had even started. Misgivings were not only creeping in, they were well established. Any conclusions we may have come to were interrupted by a German voice saying, 'Hände hoch!'

My knowledge of the language was enough to know that this meant 'Hands up!' Turning slowly we saw an old man, at least he looked old to us, pointing a double-barrelled shotgun at us and looking as though he wanted very little excuse to use it. Too old for military service, he was probably a game keeper and may have seen our tracks leading into the copse. His face seemed to light up when he realized that he had captured two escaping prisoners, not a couple of poachers. Although he did become rather nervous when, in answer to his question, we told him that our red berets signified that we were paratroopers. At the point of his gun he turned us around and we began retracing our steps.

We had no idea how many miles we had covered in the night. I suspect it was not many, owing to the frequent stops demanded by Greg. Trudging over two or three muddy fields we reached a road and here our captor steered us towards a small village about half a mile away. Having heard that news travels fast in the country, I was still surprised at the number of people who turned out to witness our humiliation. To be caught was bad enough, but to be caught by a man more than old enough to be my father was even worse. His expression showed that he was enjoying every minute of his moment of glory and I've no doubt that he dined out on the story for months afterwards.

A word from our captor to someone in the crowd sent a lad scurrying off ahead of us and I heard the word 'Polizei' (Police) mentioned. The boy had found the village Bobby at home because he emerged from a house clutching the hand of and almost dragging a large red-faced man in uniform, black or navy blue. In the policeman's house, with members of the local populace peering through the windows, we told him where we had come from, more in the hope that we would be returned there, than from any desire to co-operate.

He made a phone call and it seemed in a very short time an army lorry was at the door with an amused corporal and his interpreter. The German corporal made it plain on the return journey that he thought we were 'very silly boys.' 'With the war nearly over, why were we trying to escape?' The question didn't require an answer, he was quite right.

Back at the camp we anticipated being punished in the usual way. This would have meant being sent to a larger camp with punishment cells in which we would have been locked up for at least two weeks on bread and water. It may be that the corporal thought that our humiliation was punishment enough or that he was – by not punishing us – trying to ingratiate himself. With the war coming to its end this was possible. Alternatively, and I think this more likely, he just thought 'what the hell!' and let the matter drop. He was that kind of man. No more was said and no action was taken; we took up our lives where we had left off.

In retrospect it is my opinion that the old gamekeeper did us a large favour – however unwittingly – by capturing us. There were many stories that I heard later of our boys who having had the same idea as ourselves, met up with the Russians and were never heard of again. Some of these tales, I felt, had to be true; with the Russian troops seeing everyone in front of them as the enemy it was a question of shoot first and ask questions later! It is difficult to condemn this attitude after the horrors that the Germans had perpetrated on their advance into the Soviet Union.

It was now April 1945 and spring had arrived. It was almost like summer and of course we continued to go out to work, Greg looking like a skeleton by now. Whenever I gave him food I had to stand over him to make sure he ate it, otherwise he would have been off to the French compound trading it for tobacco. His longing for the nicotine weed had become an obsession that I found quite impossible to understand. I had smoked earlier in my life but was now glad that it hadn't the hold on me that it had on my companion.

Among our comrades were those who urged me to let him take his own road to hell, if that's the way he chose to go, and I was a survivor enough to consider it. The struggle with my conscience took time to resolve but I knew if I abandoned him I'd have to live with it for the rest of my life. Even hard-hearted Schmidt conceded that Greg was too weak to work and strode by his seated figure as if it didn't exist. He was pure bastard with the remainder of our party and never at any time considered the possibility that Germany would lose the war. The dyed-in-the-wool Nazis were mostly younger men. It was rare in my experience to find someone of Schmidt's age who thought that Hitler could do no wrong. Even at that stage, more surprisingly, Saxony was not even considered a Nazi stronghold.

Accustomed as we were to being roused at about 6 o'clock, six days a week by heavily booted sentries crying 'Raus, Raus!' it was with puzzled expressions on our faces that we sat up in bed and realized that we had been allowed to lie in one morning. This on a day when we knew we should have gone to work. Optimists amongst us suggested that the guards had buggered off now that they knew the Russians to be so close. Realists, however, felt that there was another explanation. The latter proved to be correct.

We were visited by the interpreter, practically bowing and scraping to us, his whole demeanour was nauseating as he asked us to parade outside the hut in an hour, when we would learn something to our advantage.

Curiosity had us out there long before the appointed time but we had to curb it until the corporal arrived on time with the fawning figure of the interpreter. On that beautiful sunny April day we were informed that we would no longer be required to go to work – loud cheers – and that we would sit it out until the Americans released us. There was an agreement too, that the guards would look after us until that blessed moment. Thereafter we would look after them. The 'new' prisoners showed their feelings unreservedly, I can remember, but the older ones, those who had been 'in the bag' for so long, were very subdued. It may sound ridiculous but I got the distinct feeling that some of them were not keen on going home. During the night a number of them confirmed this suspicion by going 'over the wire'. We never saw or heard of them again.

Chapter Sixteen

March to Freedom

The following day there was different and more disturbing news. Orders had been received from German High Command that we were to be kept out of Allied hands for as long as possible. In order to do this, we were officially informed that we would have to take to the road and march away from Borna. The reason for these orders, I'm sure, was that the Germans feared that at the moment of our release we would run riot in the town, looting shops, bashing up the inhabitants and raping the women. The irony of this situation didn't occur to us at once. It was when we were told that the British and French contingents only would be marching away that it hit us. The one hundred Russians were to be left behind and they were more likely to behave in this wild fashion than any of us.

Preparations were put underway immediately. Everything that could be carried was packed up, and we insisted on the Red Cross store being opened. The Germans were reluctant to do this, so one of our lads found an iron bar and simply barred off the padlock.

No wonder the Germans had been so cagey about opening it. It was almost full of parcels. Chaps like Greg had been starving and there was all this food that should have been issued to us. We were justifiably angry and the guards began to look most apprehensive. It wanted very little at that explosive point to ignite the fuse. Rightly or wrongly we felt that these parcels had been withheld with the corporal's knowledge, if not at his instigation, and any hitherto high opinion of him took a nosedive. Looking back now though, it is probable that the key to the store was in the hands of the man who did the issuing of parcels and the store was possibly full before the NCO took charge of the camp.

Determined not to leave any of this bounty to the enemy we took what we wanted for ourselves and then threw the remainder over the wire to the Russians.

With the four hundred French prisoners we took to the road; many of us were carrying far too much for a long march. The older prisoners had acquired quite a lot of kit during their long term in enemy hands and by the time we had been marching for a couple of hours much of this was dumped by the roadside. I noticed that liaisons were being formed between two or three of the guards on the one hand and the same number of men on the other. The guards were taking out insurance; they feared that the Russians reaching their homes before the Americans would have no respect for the sanctity of womanhood and rape everything female in sight. They had firm grounds for this belief but felt that with a British soldier in the house the Russians recognizing an ally would look for victims elsewhere.

Just when we felt that we were going to march all through the long April night we were halted in a village. A large barn was commandeered and we six hundred were crammed into it. With plenty of clean straw available we all settled down for an uneasy night as best we could. Come the dawn – as they say – the more observant among us noticed that the number of guards had decreased. The interpreter was one of them and he had as a companion one of the paratroopers. A couple more had departed with British soldiers as their watchdogs and who could blame them. In addition some of the guards had simply done a bunk and headed for hearth and home.

It had rained in the night but the morning was bright and clear when we formed up again. Afternoon found us approaching a town and as we got nearer we saw a slave labour camp on the outskirts.

The occupants were still under guard and locked in their compound, but they waved to us as we passed, one of them surprising us with 'it won't be long now Johnny,' as the tail of our column drew level with the gate.

We marched right through the town on its main road without learning its name. Reaching the outskirts, this time on the other side, the corporal called a halt, with the nearest houses just a few yards away and a small quarry to the right of our line of march. It was while we were resting that the town sirens began to wail, not the fluctuating sound that heralded an air raid, but a long continuous note. The noise was almost deafening and went on for five long minutes.

This we were told was the signal to warn that enemy tanks were half an hour away. Enemy tanks to the Germans meant friendly tanks to us so we greeted with pleasure the corporal's suggestion that we just sit there and wait for them. At the first real sign of an American tank the guards were to hand over their weapons to us and we would 'look after them' as previously arranged. Well, the half hour came and went, and then an hour and a little more and we were getting impatient. What had happened to our rescuers? A number of civilians approached us from the town, led by a tall man in a grey suit pushing a bicycle. Identifying the corporal as the man in charge they started a mild confab with him which quickly deteriorated into a flaming row. It ended when the NCO gave a shrug of resignation and a reluctant 'Ja'. The local people, it seemed, were afraid that if we were released by the Yanks at that spot that we would run amok in the town, looting and pillaging etc.

They were probably right. I looked at Greg and realized that he had gone as far along the road to exhaustion as possible and I still hoped that we were to be allowed to wait for the tanks to arrive. No such luck! We were ordered to our feet and just as the order was give to 'March' I bundled Greg with our belongings over the edge of the quarry. Sliding down the steep slope for about fifteen feet we hit bottom and my feet were already in motion. Grabbing Greg's arm with one hand and my kit bag with the other I started running across the floor of the quarry. There were shouts from above on the road, a cry of 'Halt' and a shot – just one. My right foot jerked under me but I kept going, panting for breath now, to a point as far as possible from the column. Diving behind a hummock of waste material overgrown with grass we lay trying to get our breathing back to normal. Greg's face was grey and he looked so dreadful that I thought perhaps my act of rescue might prove too much for him. That would have been the final irony.

More shouting on the road, recognized this time as coming from the corporal, telling the impetuous guard to control himself; a shout of 'march' and the column moved off behind some trees. A bend in the road took them completely out of our sight forever.

Chapter Seventeen

Escape and Freedom

Greg looked so ill that I felt that our best ploy was to stay where we were for the night and hope that something or someone turned up before morning. It was while I was trying in vain to get comfortable that I remembered the jerking of my right foot after we had been fired upon. A cursory inspection showed that the bullet had gone through the back of my boot at an angle coming out through the heel. Removing my boot later showed that the bullet, on its passage, had also clipped my own heel removing some of the tough skin in its flight. A close shave!

There was very little sleep for us; excitement, discomfort, concern about Greg and sirens wailing, all contributed to a very restless sight. Dawn found us saturated with the heavy dew and near the end of our tether. I was so dispirited that I became reckless. 'We've got to get out of here and get warm,' I said to Greg, hauling him to his feet. With chattering teeth we staggered back across the quarry. Was it only a few hours ago that we had foolishly launched ourselves down that slope? Well, now we had to climb the bloody thing again! It was a struggle but we made it. Not knowing what to expect I peeped over the edge to see that all was clear. There in the middle of the road was an American Jeep with three lovely big Sherman tanks behind it! The Yanks had arrived! 'Come on Greg', I said, 'it's okay', helping him to complete the last few feet with me. The men in the Jeep didn't seem to be at all surprised at our jack-in-the-box appearance from the quarry. 'Are you Arnhem boys?' one of them asked, and receiving an affirmative added, 'Here, have a drink!' He handed Greg a brown glass bottle from which he drank thirstily before passing the bottle to me. Now I'd been brought up to believe that only beer came in brown bottles so I do not know what was in that bottle, but it nearly took the top of my head off. I was gasping for breath with tears streaming down my face. One of the Americans, all concerns, stood beside me, patting me on the back and making 'there, there' noises.

As I sat down to recover, one of the tanks opened fire, and having registered a hit the others joined in. From my position on the grass I couldn't see what they were firing at so I stood up and looked down into the valley about a mile away. A large building suggesting something like a farming commune was the target. White flags of surrender were hanging from almost every window and in answer to my puzzled look one of the tank commanders shouted down one word 'sniper'. The British Army would have sent a couple of riflemen to resolve such a small problem but not the Yanks. They plastered that building until it was a heap of rubbish.

Feeling that it might help to know the name of the town, I asked one of the American officers. 'This is Colditz,' he told me. We had no idea then that the large castle imposing its brooding presence over the town was an OFLAG. More than that, we now know it held highly important officer prisoners, high-ranking civilians and officers who had repeatedly made ingenious escape attempts. None of this was known to us at that time. Had we known, a tiny bit of history would have been changed. When I asked the officer for advice on our next step, he told us to find ourselves a billet in the town and await the arrival of the supply column.

Saying our goodbyes we shook hands, and picking up the kit bag we walked the short distance to the nearby houses. Reaching the end of the main street, we were greeted by an amazing sight. The road was lined with tanks. This was one of Patton's spearheads. But the pavement on the left of the road was covered with the weary bodies of sleeping soldiers. The sound of snoring filled the air.

Thinking that one house looked as good as another, we stepped over the recumbent forms and went through the front door of the nearest dwelling. We found that it was a three-flat complex and climbed the stairs to the uppermost flat. A young couple looked startled, then afraid as we walked in, grabbed a few belongings and fled. It was not the occasion for apologies or excuses – too much had happened. Only our excitement, our exhilaration, was keeping us on our feet, but our tired bodies really longed for rest. A sudden thought occurred to me and, telling Greg that I'd only be a minute, I descended the stairs and walked into the street.

A young officer was about to rouse his men as I approached him. 'Hi,' he said with a smile reaching up to his eyes, eyes that looked as if they had seen too much. 'What can I do for you?' he added.

Not wanting to keep him from his duties too long I told him quickly of our position and asked if it was possible for us to have a couple of guns. 'No problem', said he, and walking to a Jeep reached into the well of the vehicle and came up with a Tommy-gun and a .45 Colt Automatic Pistol. It was all so casual after the strictness of the British Army, the way he handed over the weapons.

Some of the men were stirring by this time, and so making my way through them I once again ascended the stairs to the flat. Greg was asleep in a chair when I walked in so I did not disturb him. Applying the safety catches I put the weapons down on the settee.

Tired as I was, I was even hungrier so decided to investigate our own flat and the ones below if they were vacant, to see if I could find something to make a meal. Only a few biscuits and a bit of slightly mouldy cheese was all I could find in 'our' flat and nothing in the others below us. Down in the cellar I struck gold though. Shelf after shelf of bottled fruit, mainly pears and plums. They were delicious to a man starved of such luxuries for seven months and I almost ate to bursting point. Loading myself up with bottles I took them upstairs where I was surprised to find Greg on his feet. He got stuck into the fruit as well and having had his fill suggested that we have a look around outside. The weapons were lying where I had left them so I gave him the .45 and, carrying the Tommy-gun, we made our way downstairs.

There is no way that I can describe our feelings when we looked up and down the main road. It was empty. All the tanks, every man had gone. The most amazing aspect of this occurrence was that we had heard nothing. Now we were the only Allied soldiers in the town of Colditz. This was the time, had we known it, to climb the hill to the castle and release the officers imprisoned there. We did not know it though, so it didn't happen. In this way, that piece of history could have been changed. Dusk was placing its dark fingers on the town so we went back to the flat, Greg remarking on the glass scattered over the floor outside the door. He looked for a brush to sweep it up but something prompted me to suggest that it was left there.

There was just one bedroom in the flat with a large double bed in the centre. Instead of a mattress it had big bolster-type pillows lying crossways on it. They almost embraced us when we lay down. They were too comfortable.

Despite our exhaustion we could not sleep. In the early hours of the morning I thought I heard a step on the stairs but felt that I was mistaken when I heard no more. I was wide awake though when I heard footsteps crunching over the glass on the floor. Now I knew why I had asked Greg not to sweep it up. The door to the bedroom was creaking open as I reached under the bed for the Tommy-gun. Pitch black as it was, I couldn't see a thing, but the door continued to squeak as it opened further. The next sound was the cocking of a Tommy-gun as I fed a round into the breach. The intruder – if intruder it was – heeded the warning sound and ran down the stairs. It may have been the original occupiers come back to check if anyone was still in their home, we never knew.

Looking around the flat next morning we found a beautiful canteen of cutlery and were using the contents to prepare our breakfast of Red Cross biscuits, butter and jam. It was hilarious, we thought, to use a knife to spread the butter and then toss it away over a shoulder, picking up another to spread the jam. Opening a drawer, I found a sum of German money. They were notes worth millions of marks dating from around 1923 when inflation was running rampant in the Fatherland. These went into my pocket and I still have them. Discussing the subject of looting, we concluded that we would not get anything past the authorities when we arrived in England, so we didn't bother. What fools we were! After all these years, I still look back with regret at not collecting up that lovely canteen of cutlery. My mother would have loved it!

Restlessness was taking me over that morning when I stepped into the street, to see lorry after lorry marked with the large white star identifying them as Allied vehicles. The star of freedom!

These trucks made up the supply column of Patton's spearhead. Dashing back upstairs I gave Greg the news and we went down together. Our red berets were our passports to luxuries we had not seen since being captured. Those American lads could not do enough for us, plying us with tins of food, some of which heated themselves before being eaten. The temptation to add to our previously eaten scanty breakfast was too strong so we climbed the stairs again and gorged ourselves.

Later, we thought we should explore the houses further down the street and while I was in one house Greg was looking around another. When I emerged he was standing on the path with a huge grin on his face. 'Come and see what I've found,' he said excitedly. I followed him to the garage, the doors of which he'd forced open, and there stood gleaming, in all its red magnificence, a large open-topped car!

It did not require a close inspection to establish that the wheels were missing! However after further investigation inside the house, we found them in the cellar. The car was now standing on blocks of wood and having found the wheel nuts and brace in the unlocked boot, it was a simple matter to restore them to their original position on the car. We almost turned the house upside down looking for the car keys but had no luck.

At a loss and feeling frustrated I looked up and down the street and a young American Lieutenant walking along the pavement saw me and asked, 'You boys having problems?' I explained our predicament and he grinned from ear to ear. 'That's no problem'! Turning, he called out a name. 'Laurie, come here and give these boys a hand, will ya!' Laurie was a short dark staff sergeant.

He quickly assessed the situation, went to the back of a truck, and returned with tools and other mysterious gadgets. Climbing into the car he worked for about half an hour and brushing past us walked into the street again. Here he hailed one of his mates and told him to bring a Jeep and a tow-rope. 'Can't take any chances with these kraut cars, they might be booby-trapped!' says our friendly sergeant.

Hitching one end of the tow-rope to the Jeep and the other end to the car's front bumper, he reached inside the car and took up the slack. Everyone stood well back and the big red car came off its blocks as the smaller vehicle moved forward. Nothing, no bang, no anti-personnel gadget, it seemed okay. Laurie confidently climbed into the driver's seat and the words 'let's go!' had the Jeep move off to give a tow-start. Within a few yards the engine fired, caught and the car was brought to life again. 'Here you are!' grinned Laurie. 'Drive it around for a while to top up the battery'.

We were getting into the car to act on his advice when we saw yet another Yank approaching with large stencils in the shape of a star. He painted a small one on each door and larger ones on the bonnet and the boot lid transforming the car into a liberated vehicle. The petrol tank had been filled too. While this was being done, we were overwhelmed by all this kindness. We were as excited as kids in a Christmas grotto and made our way slowly down the main street of Colditz.

A drunken Yank, barely able to stand, was on a corner near a watch-seller's shop. He was waving a Tommy-gun under the nose of a very frightened German soldier. It was only minutes, I thought, before the GI pulls the trigger, accidentally or otherwise.

Stopping the car I got out, with my own Tommy-gun hanging by its trigger guard from my right forefinger. 'Let me do it!' I said to the drunk. Barely able to see, he blinked owlishly in an attempt to focus. It was the red beret that helped; he fixed his eyes on it and asked, 'You an Arnhem boy?' I nodded. 'You have him then and do it good,' replied he, stepping away from his intended victim. Looking as if I meant business, I moved my gun in the direction of a nearby alley indicating that the enemy soldier should precede me. By now he was as white as a sheet. No doubt thinking that while his captor had changed, he was no better off.

In the alley I told the German to get into the nearest house and change into civilian clothes. Not quite believing his luck he scuttled off as I fired two shots into the air for effect. Greg was still sitting in the passenger seat. He looked at me and said three words: 'you rotten bastard!' Only when I drove past the end of the alley did he accept my protestation that I had not shot down a man in cold blood.

The whole unpleasant episode had dampened our exhilaration somewhat so we made our way back to the flat. About to walk up the path we were stopped by the young lieutenant, who told us that the column was moving on in an hour. He opened a map and quickly showed us a route to an airfield where, he said, Dakotas were flying out with PoWs. Then he went on to say that if we were able to stick to the American lines all the way through Germany and France we would probably be allowed to take the car to England on a tank landing craft. This was an alternative worth considering.

If we took the latter option, he assured us, there'd be plenty of petrol en route to help us on our way. Assuming that we knew what he was talking about, he added 'oh by the way, don't worry about those guys in the castle, somebody has already been up there!' Seeing the puzzlement on our faces he enlightened us, but the significance of his news didn't hit us until much later.

The people from the slave labour camp had been turned loose by the advancing spearhead and they were going mad. Their new found freedom was a heady stimulant. Shops were broken into and looted, more cars appeared on the streets driven by ex-prisoners, and screams from nearby houses clearly indicated that women were being violated. To our shame we just shrugged our shoulders and said, 'What the hell?' All we really wanted was to get home.

The supply column departed, leaving us as the only Allied soldiers on the street, in possession of the town. Perhaps the responsibility was too much for us both: we decided to leave as well and made plans for that afternoon. Studying the map the officer had given us, a German map to our surprise, we noticed that the route we had to take lay through Borna. The agreement to pay Herr Schmidt a visit was unanimous. Before that though, there were other adventures.

With the urge to travel homewards very strong in us, we had an early and hurried lunch. On the point of leaving the flat with our few belongings I remembered seeing a silver fox-fur muff in the bedroom and ran back to get it. I had a girl-friend at home and wished to surprise her with an unusual gift. Only later when I examined it more closely did I find that it was a purse as well.

Slinging our kit onto the back seat of the car, we started up and took the road over which we had wearily marched so short a time before. So short a time, yet so much had happened in that time.

Entering a small town near dusk we were greeted by the sight of a Tiger tank, a smoking hulk at the side of the road. A body was sprawled half in, half out of the turret and most of the crew were scattered about, obviously shot down as they attempted to escape the burning Tiger. An American soldier in shirt sleeves was on point duty at a crossroads. He had wrist watches all the way up both arms. He hailed us and, obviously used to dealing with PoWs homeward bound, directed us to a hotel where he suggested we spend the night. There his sense of hospitality ended. When asked if he had a wrist watch to spare, his reply was succinct and ended with 'off!'

His eyes were clearly on our car but if he had any notions about making a trade for any or all of his watches we quickly dispelled them by driving away, leaving him standing there in our dust. Another Yank directed us to the guarded car park in the rear of the hotel, where once again the car became the object of close scrutiny, one GI saying, 'I'd sure like to drive down the main street back home in that baby!'

Delightful smells of cooking food greeted us as we entered the foyer of the hotel. There were tables laid end to end covering most of the floor, with a passage between leading to the stairs. Some of the diners were American serving with the unit then in possession of the town, but by far the greater number were, like ourselves, ex-prisoners on their way home.

The complete informality of it all impressed us and I wondered if we would have experienced the same level of hospitality had we been moving through British lines. I think not. Even when we enquired which room we should take, we were told, 'just find an empty one and it's yours!'

I slept better that night than I had for a long, long time and was brushing my teeth next morning over the wash basin when I heard a shot, just one! It sounded quite close to the hotel and I could hear shouting out in the street but had no idea what had happened at that stage. Some careless Yank probably loosing off a round accidentally was one thought. It was later we learned the full story. Breakfast was calling – the smell of frying bacon had been wafting upstairs for some time. Descending the stairs we saw a large bundle covered with canvas on a table and thought that it was food stuff awaiting removal to the kitchen. Breakfast would not have gone down so well, had we known what was under that canvas.

An American officer asked us if we spoke any German. Not knowing why he was asking I told him that we'd only been 'in the bag' for seven months, but yes, we did speak a little of the native tongue. 'We have a POW cage here,' he said, 'None of my men speak German at all, so could you help us out?' After the way we had been treated by these chaps, kindness without reservation, I could only agree to do so and was driven to the barbed wire enclosure where a large number of Germans were incarcerated.

Try to picture the figure I presented to these men. On my head was my Red Beret with the Recce Squadron badge over my left eye, an American shirt with collar, hand-made tie around my neck, covered by the waterproof jacket which had served me so well throughout the harsh winter. Round my waist was a German Army leather belt with 'Gott Mit Uns' buckle, and a leather holster complete with 9mm pistol which I had acquired in the town of Colditz. Below this I was wearing my clean khaki British Army trousers with a smart crease. Completing the ensemble were a pair of highly polished boots and my webbing gaiters. Somewhere along the way I had acquired a walking stick too and this seemed to give an air of authority.

A row of recently captured Germans was formed up outside the cage and I was asked to order them to empty their pockets and tip out their rucksacks onto the grass. Whereas before my arrival, I was told, these men had maintained their arrogant attitudes towards their captors, they were now quite respectful. I don't know why. I can't explain it, at 5ft 7¼ inches I hardly presented a commanding figure. Giving instructions in my limited German I walked along the line, occasionally flicking disdainfully at some item with my walking stick.

A ribald cheer went up from the prisoners already in the cage and, turning, I saw an American sergeant with a Tommy-gun in the crook of his right arm pushing ahead of him an attractive blonde girl in civilian clothes. Only yards away from where we stood, there was a deep dry ditch and, forcing her into this, he followed her. Rape was clearly on his mind and equally clearly, that is what followed, judging by the sounds coming from the ditch. Throughout these proceedings the captives kept up their derisive cat-calling but these were silenced by the sound of a shot from the cleft in the ground. My first reaction was a feeling of utter disgust. Conquering heroes who shoot women, and unarmed women at that, were very low in my opinion. However, the full story then emerged. The sergeant climbed up to our level and said defensively: 'that bitch shot my buddy this morning!'

This was the shot that we had heard earlier. She had been caught red-handed in the spire of the local church with a rifle in her hands. There is no doubt, now, in my mind, that had she been handed over to the proper authorities she may possibly have served a couple of years before being freed to continue her life. I'm sure, too that she had counted on this, but the dead man's friend had acted as judge, jury and ultimately executioner after he had exacted his own payment. The bundle, of course, lying on the table, was the woman's victim.

With the number of prisoners dwindling as the front – such as it was – got further and further away, we decided to move on. After two days we headed for Borna and arrived there in the afternoon of a lovely spring day following a leisurely breakfast and lunch.

Knowing that the name Schmidt was a very common one in Germany we anticipated difficulty in locating our erstwhile boss.

In the wake of speeding Patton, Borna was struggling for some restoration of normality. There were a number of ex-PoWs walking around on the main street and when we asked a couple of them what they were doing about food, were told, 'just walk in and help yourself!' This apparently applied to shops or houses, but we just hadn't the gall to do this. Anyway we were not in danger of going hungry. We'd been supplied with provisions before leaving the previous town. Our American friends seemed to have a very high regard for Arnhem veterans and couldn't do enough for us.

Walking into a nearby shop I was greeted with some apprehension by the proprietor standing in front of me wringing his hands. He'd already been visited by a number of ex-Kriegies who had simply taken what they wanted from his meagre stock.

There was bread and cheese on display and he assumed that we had come to relieve him of some more. When I assured him that I was enquiring about the whereabouts of a German ganger named Schmidt his relief was pathetic. Telling me that he couldn't help me he scurried out of his store and into one next door. We followed and heard a gabbled conversation in very fast dialect which was well beyond our capacity to understand.

It transpired that while there were a great number of Schmidt's in Borna there was only one who had been a ganger on the open-cast coal mine and everyone knew him as a fervent Nazi. Following the directions we were given and having to stop a couple of times to ask again, we came to the house, clean and tidy in a neat street. Carrying our weapons we walked up the path to the front door.

The door was opened so quickly in answer to our knock, we suspected that Schmidt had been waiting in the hall. Recognizing us at once, he held out his right hand. I ignored it. Putting on a brave face he said in his broken English, 'Ah Steffans, I'm glad to see you are well!' Two attractive blonde heads appeared through the doorway leading into the front room and Greg and I had the idea at the same time. At that stage our only intention was to humiliate this man who had driven us hard at work. Rape or sex in any form was not, definitely not, on our minds. Taking a girl each by the arm we started to lead them upstairs and whilst we were within sight and sound of their father they put up a fair imitation of daughters who were being wrongfully treated. When we turned the bend in the stairs, however, it was an altogether different matter. They took the initiative and practically dragged us into their separate bedrooms.

We stayed an hour and Greg looked paler than ever when he emerged. Schmidt was standing in the hall by the open door and his face was like stone as we left his house. Justice, we thought, had been served, as had his daughters!

Eagerness to get home helped us to make our next decision and that was to head for the airfield from whence we could get a plane to England. Out came the map again and we saw that we hadn't far to go. The airfield, we noticed on our arrival, was surrounded by gentle hills rising and falling in the afternoon sun. Ex-prisoners had apparently been arriving on all forms of transport, but none had driven up to the gate in a large red German car. It aroused quite a lot of comment. Having been directed to an office building we parked and went inside. Here we were asked for name, rank, number and unit and then were given a cardboard tag with a number on it. 'You are at the end of the queue,' we were told, 'but when you hear that number called on the tannoy, come running!'

This was an ex-German Airforce field into which Dakotas were flying taxi fashion to take out wounded personnel. The number of wounded not being as great as anticipated, fortunately, meant that they had space to carry out ex-PoWs. In the free and easy fashion we'd now come to expect from the Yanks, we were told to find our own billets. The one we found was ideal. It was a small two-bedded room with another next door, the outside wall of which had been blown down in a bombing raid. It made an excellent garage for the car when we had cleared away the rubble.

Nights were very quiet but during the day we could hear distant shots and thought that perhaps the GIs were doing some mopping-up in the area. Two or three days had passed when we were approached by a number of officers and NCOs on the staff of the airfield.

That was surprise enough, sitting outside the billet as we were, waiting for our numbers to be called. A greater surprise came when an American captain said, 'have you boys heard the shooting that's been taking place during the day?' Naturally we had to admit that we had and that we had wondered who had been doing the shooting. 'There are snipers in the hills,' we were told, 'We are here to ask you if you boys will do something about it for us?'

Explaining more fully he told us that the troops running the airfield were specialists and did their own particular jobs very well but that they had had very little or no infantry training. Weapons suitable for the job would be supplied if we were prepared to take it on. Greg was ruled out immediately because of his condition; he still looked very gaunt. The short time he had been eating better meals had made no noticeable difference to his appearance.

I chose a long-range sniper's rifle with a telescopic sight and was able to try it out on the shooting butts already in the grounds of the airstrip. Four ex-PoWs including myself had volunteered for this distasteful task. One was from a Scottish regiment and the other two were Paras. Our natural reluctance to wander off into the wilds to catch or kill men we couldn't at that moment see was overcome somewhat when we were told that three men had been killed and a number wounded. A Jeep was put at our disposal and, as a member of the Recce Squadron, I was delegated to drive it. My pay book showed that I was a first class shot and I confess to having a certain pride in my expertise with the infantryman's principal weapon – the rifle.

With no information at all as to the exact or even approximate position of the snipers, we just swanned off into the blue. In three days we nailed one of them. Patrolling in pairs, the Scot and one Para, me and the other Para, it was the Scot who got one lined up and without any finesse, let him have it. There was no more trouble after that. The others, if there were more, lost heart and faded away. It was rather hairy though, while it lasted.

Seven days had gone by, waiting to fly home. The weather was deteriorating too and on this day it was pouring down with rain – I mean really pouring down, and blowing half a gale. Not the day for flying we thought, and had no sooner formed the thought when the door burst open and a soaked, bedraggled GI stepped into our room. 'Are you guys Evans and Gregory?' he asked. We nodded when he quoted our numbers too. 'Well, get the lead out. There's a plane waiting for you on the strip. You're the last two on board!'

No one but a lunatic would fly in such conditions, was our opinion, strongly worded. 'If you don't get this one, you'll go to the end of the queue again!' our friend riposted. Grabbing our few things we were ready to brave the elements when I remembered something. 'Do you want a car?' He looked puzzled. 'What's a car?' I recalled that our two great nations were separated by a common language. 'Do you want an AUTOMOBILE?' I corrected, leading him into the corridor and along to the next room cum garage. Flinging open the door I said 'it's yours!' We left him jumping up and down with joy and his cries of 'yippee!' told us he'd forgotten how wet he was.

There was no doubt about which was our plane. It was the only one on the strip with its props turning. Dashing through the blinding rain we managed to scramble aboard, the door was closed and we were on our way. Destination Brussels. The RAF, we had learned, were to fly us home after we had been through a transit camp in the Belgian capital. The back of the queue again, but we didn't mind that – we could rough it in Brussels for a few days.

With eager anticipation we were lifted into the sky. It was, without fear of contradiction, the worst bloody flight I've ever known. Hoping to fly under the weather the pilot was skipping over the hills. It was like being in a lift that had run amok, only more so. Two of the passengers were violently air sick, and I was one of them. This had never happened to me before. Stomachs had settled down however before landing, but instead of the eagerly awaited sojourn in Brussels we were shown, one by one, into a large marquee.

DDT was squirted up trouser legs and down collars, then we were pointed towards a waiting Lancaster Bomber. The authorities, realizing that an empty plane was standing on the airfield, thought that we might just as well get on board rather than be driven to the camp and another batch of men brought out. No doubt they felt that they were doing us a favour but after only seven months captivity we were ready for a taste of the high life.

The trip in the Lancaster was as smooth as silk, and for most of the way I was standing in the astrodome at the invitation of the navigator.

We landed in fine weather, at Horsham in Sussex. We were shown – by pretty WAAFs – into a huge hangar where tables were laid out with white table cloths and heaped with food, including white bread. It looked strange. Greg and I sat at the same table and were eating some of the sandwiches when a very pretty WAAF officer sat down opposite me. She exchanged a few pleasantries initially, and then asked, 'Have you brought home any souvenirs?' Rather proudly I produced the silver fox fur muff and told her that it was for my girl-friend. Then to my astonishment she blatantly propositioned me: her sexual favour in exchange for the muff. I wasn't even tempted, pretty or not. I'd never paid for sex in my life and was not about to start now and told her so. She went off in a fit of pique.

From the hangar we went into a large Nissen hut where an Army colonel addressed us. The very first thing he said to us was, 'I don't care what you've got; we are not going to take a thing off you!' Those words have echoed in mind for over forty years and when I heard them I wanted to get the next plane back. Too late, too late! The colonel told us that, regardless of how long we had been prisoners, we were all to be given six weeks leave and therefore would be kitted out sufficiently for that period. A quick trip to the kit store and then to the camp tailors. They must have worked all night: our uniforms were ready next morning, perfect fit for me, complete with all my Airborne Insignia. Leave passes, for appropriate destinations; Greg and I exchanged addresses and we were driven to the nearest railway stations.

An uneventful journey via London to Liverpool, but only when I was halfway up the street and our little Scottie dog came bounding towards me did I accept that I was finally home.

My weight when I was captured was 10 stone 7 pounds. On arrival home I weighed myself and found that I was 8 stone 2 pounds. A loss of 33 pounds. Had I not been such a good forager determined to survive, it would have been much more I'm sure.

I never saw or heard from Greg again! Perhaps when he had recovered he reflected how, during his seven months in German hands, his addiction to and obsession for tobacco had almost killed him. I was a witness to his degradation and he probably thought it was best forgotten. For my part, I felt that in getting him home, my responsibility was ended. I can never see him – in my imagination – as the fine figure of a man he once was, always as the wasted, yellow-faced creature as I last saw him. I'd be amazed, surprised and yes delighted of course to have learned that he was still alive.

Des Evan ex-Trooper C Troop 1st Airborne Recce Sqn, finished this day 27 March 1988.

Epilogue

Throughout the 1980s, 90s and up until 2002 I was a regular visitor at Des and Betty's. When I had business calls in Norfolk, I would ensure that my last call on a Friday put me near enough to West Runton so that I could stay with them, leaving for home on the Sunday. We met in Oosterbeek year on year and they in turn came to stay with my wife and me in the North West. We telephoned each other at least a couple of times a month and letters flowed between us on a weekly basis. When I collected his archive into my safekeeping I found he had kept every single letter I had ever written to him…truly remarkable!

I had been training to be a Registered Nurse for about a year when I visited Des and Betty in 1998. Des explained that he had been experiencing some troublesome symptoms – which to me even with my relative inexperience – had all the hallmarks of Type 2 or Maturity Onset Diabetes. Sure enough a visit to his doctor and some simple tests confirmed this. Des's lifestyle was quite disciplined. He didn't drink much (a small glass of wine or beer was as much as I ever saw him consume), he didn't smoke, he took regular long brisk walks daily, and their diet was enviable: home cooked fresh food with plenty of fruit and vegetables. Therefore there was little or nothing Des could have done to change his lifestyle and control his diabetes in that way. Clearly he would need medication. Now whether or not he ever did receive medication or whether he ever took it, I cannot say.

What is clear is that by 2000, he was starting to exhibit signs of vascular dementia (a complication often associated with poorly controlled diabetes). His memory was starting to show signs of being compromised. Letters remained unanswered.

My wife and I visited them both at home, but we'd already agreed that we would camp at nearby Beeston Regis, so as not to burden them with guests. As usual they were happy to see us both and we were equally happy to see them. However both my wife and I were somewhat shocked by the change in Des. Clearly there were problems.

The 60th anniversary of the Battle of Arnhem was marked in 2004. I telephoned Des to tell him that I was making the pilgrimage to Arnhem that year (I had no illusions that he would go). I recall he seemed vague on the telephone, unsure about what I was telling him. I promised to telephone when I returned. The 60th pilgrimage was truly memorable. I went with a group of extremely enthusiastic chaps whose one motivation was to keep the memory alive of all those who fought in the battle. Because of my close associations with Des, I was privileged to be asked to deliver a small lecture at the site of the 'Tuesday Ambush' and to recount Des's part in that encounter. I returned from Arnhem and telephoned Des, who, though interested, again seemed vague in his responses.

Towards the end of October 2004, I had this all-pervading feeling that something was wrong! I couldn't put my finger on it. I had this strange compulsion to ring Des to make sure he and Betty were alright. I recall trying repeatedly, the telephone constantly ringing out unanswered. I knew they could not have gone away. Des was no longer driving, Betty was becoming increasingly infirm. I eventually hit on the idea of obtaining the telephone number of their neighbour via directory enquiries. Success. He answered and told me the sad news that acting on the concerns from Social Services, a Social Worker accompanied by the police had arrived at Des and Betty's and had taken Betty off to Hospital in Norwich whilst Des had been handcuffed and taken to the Julian Hospital under a Section of the Mental Health Act.

I was distraught. I telephoned the hospital and ascertained that Betty was well – given her frailty – and was awaiting placement in a nursing or residential home. I made contact with the Julian Hospital who explained Des was comfortable but remained under the 'Section'.

I immediately made plans to visit and recall setting off in appalling weather – thick fog – all the way. I found some digs in Norwich and went straight to the Julian. I was allowed in without ceremony, having explained who I was, where I had travelled from and my relationship with Des. Although I was shocked by his appearance, gaunt, his hair longer than I had ever seen, I was encouraged that he recognized me immediately throwing his arms around me and giving me a big hug. We were allowed to chat in private and it was then I realized how affected his mind had become, with little or no recollection of events past or present. As I was about to leave, another patient wandered into the room and began to interrupt our conversation. Des, without warning, literally launched himself at this chap and pinned him up against a wall. I managed to persuade Des to let him go – which he did – and the other patient wandered off. I said goodbye and then went off and spoke to the charge nurse. He told me Des had actually escaped from the hospital, which had resulted in a man-hunt of several hours involving a police helicopter.

I explained something of Des's past to the nurse in an attempt to explain exactly why Des would feel compelled to escape – instinct! I'm not convinced it had any impact at all on the member of staff. I then went on to visit Betty in the Hospital. I was able to tell Betty I'd seen Des and that he appeared well. To me Betty – although frail – seemed much as I'd remembered her. I stayed until the end of patient visiting and then went and got a meal and back to the digs.

I sat for hours in my room that night composing a letter to the Julian asking them to consider the placement of Des in combined Enduring Mental Illness home so that he and Betty could be together. I now know that due to Des's unpredictable and often violent behaviour, nowhere suitable could be found, despite every effort.

I woke the following morning, visited Betty, and then went onto see Des; we spent some time together before I said goodbye. It would be the last time I would see either of them alive. The years passed, I telephoned Betty in her nursing home in Mundesley on a regular basis. She was always pleased to hear from me, as I was to hear her voice. I contacted the home where Des was residing, enquiring how he was and if it would be possible to visit him. The response was predictable. He would not engage with anyone, was at times violent, and they didn't want me to waste my time making a fruitless journey. I felt complete despair after these phone calls.

In June 2010 I received the fateful letter: Des – after a disturbed night – had been found dead in his room by one of the care home staff the following morning. The coroner's report apparently said cause of death: pneumonia. I felt a part of my heart had been ripped out! I contacted Betty's cousin Pam who was making the funeral arrangements. Pam was very understanding and realized how much Des had meant to me and asked me what sort of funeral service Des would have liked and would I like to help with this. I readily agreed.

The funeral was arranged for 1 July 2010. I made my way down to Norwich the night before and met up with another close friend of mine and an acquaintance of Des, Mr Nick Clark. With that terrible dread that one experiences on the morning of the funeral of a much loved friend, we made our way to Norwich Crematorium. To my complete amazement, there was an honour guard from the Parachute Regiment Association, including two standard bearers.

Nick had brought the 1st Airborne Recce Squadron Old Comrades Association standard as well.

The hearse arrived. His coffin was covered with the Union Flag. I put his old red beret on his coffin, a last tribute to a soldier. He was carried inside and I walked behind his coffin. I like to think he would have been pleased with the tributes and the service. Old friends and neighbours, the standards, stirring hymns – including his and my favourite, 'Abide with me'. I delivered my tribute to a much loved friend, I fought back the tears. As the curtains cloaked his coffin, I bowed and said goodbye my friend.

In 2013 I was contacted by Pam. Arrangements had finally been made to inter both Betty and Des's ashes. It was to take place on Saturday, 30 November at the Parish Church of Mundesley. I made the journey down to Norfolk. Driving down the A148 I passed the turning to 'Sandy Lane' West Runton; I resisted the very real temptation to detour and visit the cottage. I made my way to Mundesley; the sun was shining with the occasional rain squall. It was bitterly cold. The appointed time arrived and in convoy we made our way to the parish church. My friend Nick Clark had again made the journey from Essex and had brought the Recce Corps standard as a final tribute for Des.

We assembled around a small square hole. Prayers and readings were said and finally they were both laid to rest, together on a beautiful cliff top overlooking the North Sea. After everyone else had gone, I gazed out across the sea and thought, 'just across the water is Holland – where 29 years ago we met'. I paid my final respects and left them together, just as they would have wanted. Till we meet again old friend!

The End